CliffsNotes™
Understanding
Health
Insurance

By Darlene Brill

D1562518

IN THIS BOOK

- Get acquainted with the key elements of your health insurance plan
- Know your options when you may lose your health insurance
- Assess your need for supplemental insurance
- Make sense of Medicare and Medicaid requirements and benefits
- Understand your consumer rights and responsibilities
- Reinforce what you learn with CliffsNotes Review
- Find more health insurance information in CliffsNotes Resource Center and online at www.cliffsnotes.com

IDG Books Worldwide, Inc.
An International Data Group Company
Foster City, CA • Chicago, IL • Indianapolis, IN • New York, NY

IDG
BOOKS
WORLDWIDE

About the Author

Darlene Brill cut her teeth in the insurance industry by processing claims for a self-insured employer, well before the advent of HMOs and PPOs. Her ventures into the health insurance maze have been from the perspective of both group and private plans.

Publisher's Acknowledgments

Editorial

Project Editors: Christine Meloy Beck, Mary Goodwin

Acquisitions Editors: Mark Butler, Karen Hansen

Senior Copy Editor: Tamara Castleman

Technical Reviewers: L. Peter Leone, II; Terri Raffin

Production

Proofreader: Vickie Broyles

Indexer: Johnna VanHoose

IDG Books Indianapolis Production Department

CliffsNotes™ Understanding Health Insurance

Published by

IDG Books Worldwide, Inc.

An International Data Group Company

919 E. Hillsdale Blvd.

Suite 400

Foster City, CA 94404

www.idgbooks.com (IDG Books Worldwide Web site)

www.cliffsnotes.com (CliffsNotes Web site)

Library of Congress Catalog Card No.: 99-64867

ISBN: 0-7645-8514-2

Printed in the United States of America

10 9 8 7 6 5 4 3 2 1

1O/TR/QY/ZZ/IN

Distributed in the United States by IDG Books Worldwide, Inc.

Distributed by CDG Books Canada Inc. for Canada; by Transworld Publishers Limited in the United Kingdom; by IDG Norge Books for Norway; by IDG Sweden Books for Sweden; by IDG Books Australia Publishing Corporation Pty. Ltd. for Australia and New Zealand; by TransQuest Publishers Pte Ltd. for Singapore, Malaysia, Thailand, Indonesia, and Hong Kong; by Gotop Information Inc. for Taiwan; by ICG Muse, Inc. for Japan; by Norma Comunicaciones S.A. for Colombia; by Intersoft for South Africa; by Eyrolles for France; by International Thomson Publishing for Germany, Austria and Switzerland; by Distribuidora Cuspide for Argentina; by LR International for Brazil; by Ediciones ZETA S.C.R. Ltda. for Peru; by WS Computer Publishing Corporation, Inc., for the Philippines; by Contemporanea de Ediciones for Venezuela; by Express Computer Distributors for the Caribbean and West Indies; by Micronesia Media Distributor, Inc. for Micronesia; by Grupo Editorial Norma S.A. for Guatemala; by Chips Computadoras S.A. de C.V. for Mexico; by Editorial Norma de Panama S.A. for Panama; by American Bookshops for Finland. Authorized Sales Agent: Anthony Rudkin Associates for the Middle East and North Africa.

For general information on IDG Books Worldwide's books in the U.S., please call our Consumer Customer Service department at **800-762-2974**. For reseller information, including discounts and premium sales, please call our Reseller Customer Service department at **800-434-3422**.

For information on where to purchase IDG Books Worldwide's books outside the U.S., please contact our International Sales department at 317-596-5530 or fax **317-596-5692**.

For consumer information on foreign language translations, please contact our Customer Service department at **1-800-434-3422**, fax **317-596-5692**, or e-mail rights@idgbooks.com.

For information on licensing foreign or domestic rights, please phone +1-650-655-3109.

For sales inquiries and special prices for bulk quantities, please contact our Sales department at 650-655-3200 or write to the address above.

For information on using IDG Books Worldwide's books in the classroom or for ordering examination copies, please contact our Educational Sales department at **800-434-2086** or fax **317-596-5499**.

For press review copies, author interviews, or other publicity information, please contact our Public Relations department at **650-655-3000** or fax **650-655-3299**.

For authorization to photocopy items for corporate, personal, or educational use, please contact Copyright Clearance Center, 222 Rosewood Drive, Danvers, MA 01923, or fax **978-750-4470**.

Table of Contents

INTRODUCTION

Whatever your particular circumstances, when you or a family member needs medical treatment, you may not have the time to research what you need to know about health insurance. So the more you understand ahead of time, the better prepared you are in a serious medical situation.

Why Do You Need This Book?

Can you answer yes to any of these questions?

- Do you need to learn about health insurance fast?

- Do you not have the time to read 500 pages on health insurance?

- Do you want to feel more confident when dealing with health insurance administrators and health care providers?

- Do you want the know-how to get the greatest benefit from your health insurance plan?

If so, then CliffsNotes *Understanding Health Insurance* is for you!

How to Use This Book

This book provides a condensed, practical guide through the health insurance maze. You can read this book straight through or just look for the information you need. You can find information on a particular topic in a number of ways: You can search the index in the back of the book, locate your topic in the Table of Contents, or read the In This Chapter list in each chapter.

To reinforce your learning, check out the Review and the Resource Center at the back of the book. To help you find important information in the book, look for the following icons in the text:

A Remember icon points out information that's worth keeping in mind.

This icon highlights helpful hints or advice.

This icon alerts you to situations you want to avoid.

Don't Miss Our Web Site

Keep up with the changing world of insurance by visiting the CliffsNotes Web site at www.cliffsnotes.com. Here's what you find:

- Interactive tools that are fun and informative
- Links to interesting Web sites
- Additional resources to help you continue your learning

At www.cliffsnotes.com, you can even register for a new feature called CliffsNotes Daily, which offers you newsletters on a variety of topics, delivered right to your e-mail inbox each business day.

If you haven't yet discovered the Internet and are wondering how to get online, pick up *Getting on the Internet*, new from CliffsNotes. You'll learn just what you need to make your online connection quickly and easily. See you at www.cliffsnotes.com!

CHAPTER 1

EVALUATING YOUR HEALTH INSURANCE PLAN

IN THIS CHAPTER

- Getting insurance on your own or through a group
- Understanding the differences in types of managed care plans
- Learning about traditional fee-for-service plans
- Continuing coverage with COBRA

This chapter gives you an understanding of the major features of each type of plan, such as fee-for-service, HMO, and PPO. As you read, refer often to the Checklist in Chapter 10. The Checklist is a tool to help you keep tabs on what features of health insurance plans are important to you. For details and exact provisions, always read the specific policies, contract, and/or plan document; follow up with questions to your plan administrator and state insurance agency.

To get the most from this chapter, know the following definitions:

- **Deductible:** The amount of covered charges that you must pay before the insurance company will pay any benefits.

- **Coinsurance:** The set percentage of covered charges that you must pay after you have met (paid) the deductible.

■ **Copayment:** A fixed fee that you must pay each time you use a specified service. Sometimes called an *encounter fee.*

Note: Some discussions of health insurance use the terms *copayment* and *coinsurance* interchangeably. This book uses *copayment* as a fixed dollar amount and *coinsurance* as a fixed percentage of a fee.

Group Health Insurance Plans

Most people in the United States are covered by a health insurance plan that their employer or a family member's employer offers. Often the employer pays a portion or all of the insurance's cost. Many other people are members of groups — such as unions, professional associations, religious or veterans' organizations, fraternal groups, and organizations of entrepreneurs or small businesses — that have contracts with insurance companies to provide health care coverage.

To qualify for a group plan, you must meet the sponsoring organization's or association's eligibility requirements. For example, you may have to work a minimum number of hours weekly to participate in the plan.

Enrolling in a group plan has several advantages. You may be able to choose from among several plans that your employer offers. The cost of premiums is usually lower because of the large number of participants. If you enroll when you are first eligible to do so — such as when you start a job, when you experience a *life status change* (as defined by the IRS), or during an *open enrollment period* (an interval during which members of a plan can change health plans or coverage) — neither you nor your spouse or dependents have to provide evidence of insurability (see Chapter 3 for more information). In a group plan, you can't be excluded or charged a premium that is higher than that of the rest of the group.

Individual Health Insurance Plans

If your group plan doesn't meet all your health insurance needs or if you don't have access to a group health insurance plan, your only choice — other than paying for all medical expenses yourself — may be to purchase an individual health insurance plan.

When you select a plan, whether individual or group, avoid surprises: Carefully read the policy, contract, and/or plan document and make sure that you understand it. Before you purchase the plan, confirm that it includes a *free-look clause.* Many insurance companies include this clause, which gives you at least ten days to review the policy after you receive it. If you choose to return the policy, the company will refund your premium.

Buying an individual plan

You can buy individual health insurance plans from an insurance agent or broker or directly from the insurance company. Start with the agent or broker who handles your car, life, homeowner's, or renter's insurance. Ask friends, neighbors, and work associates about their agents. Check out at least three agents. Call insurance companies, HMOs, and PPOs (see "Managed Care Plans," later in this chapter) directly. Use the Yellow Pages in your telephone directory as a source for names of insurance companies. Look under the heading "Insurance" for entries that mention health insurance. Search the Internet or check out insurance company Web sites. If you don't have a specific type of health plan in mind, ask the company representative to explain the types and cost of plans the company sells.

Applying for and enrolling in an individual plan

When you leave a job, most group plans allow you to continue your coverage with the same benefits under COBRA (discussed in detail later in this chapter). You may also be able to convert your group plan to an individual plan, which may offer benefits that differ from the group benefits. The advantage of this option is continuity of coverage. You don't have to repeat the enrollment process, so you won't have to qualify or worry about a waiting period based on a *pre-existing condition* (a medical condition that is actively being treated during the application process). See more about pre-existing conditions in Chapter 3.

When you apply for coverage in an individual plan, be prepared to answer many questions in detail about your medical history and the history of family members you want to cover. You may have to take a physical and/or release medical records to the insurance company. Depending on your (or a dependent's) health condition, an insurance company may write a plan that excludes a pre-existing condition, or the company may charge a higher premium for the policy.

Understanding costs

Don't be surprised at the much higher price and lower benefits (including prescription benefits) of an individual plan — you don't have the advantage of group clout. However, in an effort to keep costs down, you may be able to work with the insurance company to customize a plan that fits your specific needs. For example, you can choose a higher deductible to lower your premium costs.

With a *noncancellable policy,* your coverage continues as long as you keep paying the monthly premium. Under this type of policy, the insurance company can increase your premiums but can't cancel your coverage. Another type of policy is a *conditionally renewable policy.* This qualification allows an insurance company to cancel all policies similar to yours but protects your policy from being individually selected for termination.

Resorting to a high-risk health insurance pool

In some cases, insurers may consider you a high risk, perhaps because of a pre-existing condition. If you can't get health insurance anywhere, you may be eligible for your state's *high-risk pool.*

High-risk pools make health insurance available to everyone, regardless of their health. Costs are high, coverage may be minimal, and you may have to pay higher deductibles and coinsurance, so consider this type of coverage only after you exhaust other possibilities. The structure of high-risk pools varies from state to state, so be sure to check with your state's insurance department for specific information. (The Resource Center at the end of this book lists the address, telephone numbers, and Web site address for the National Association of Insurance Commissioners, which helps you find your state health insurance contact.) If you want to insure dependents who aren't high risk, finding another health insurance plan is much more economical.

Fee-for-Service Plans

Fee-for-service health insurance plans (also known as *indemnity plans*) are what people think of as traditional health plans: Insurance companies pay the fees for covered services, generally after you pay a deductible. This type of plan allows you to choose any doctor, and you can change doctors at any time. You can go to any hospital, anywhere in the country. This type of plan is more common in individual policies than in group policies. Fee-for-service policies usually offer *comprehensive coverage,* a combination of *basic coverage* and *major medical coverage.*

Basic coverage

Basic coverage includes benefits for expenses you incur during a hospital stay, such as

- **Hospitalization,** including room and board and regular nursing services during the hospital stay

- **Other hospital charges,** such as inpatient X rays, lab tests, anesthesia, supplies, and medications

- **Surgical expenses,** including surgeons' charges and other charges for surgery both inpatient and outpatient

- **Physician expenses,** including visits to the doctor's office and visits the doctor makes to the patient at home or in the hospital

Note: This plan may not cover preventive care, such as checkups, so you may have to pay these expenses yourself.

You usually receive benefits during a hospital stay for a set number of days; the plan also has a maximum amount that it pays per day. In both cases, you're likely to be responsible for the balance. A plan may pay for extended home care for a short time or not at all. Some plans don't pay for prescription expenses.

Some indemnity plans pay a fixed amount to the provider or to the insured person, regardless of the amount charged for the actual expense. *Scheduled plans* set a maximum amount they pay for each service. These amounts reflect the *reasonable and customary* — also called *usual and customary* — fees for such services in the same geographic area in which they are provided. (See Chapter 2 for more on reasonable and customary fees.) You may have to pay the difference in cost — in addition to the deductible and coinsurance you've already paid — between what your provider charges and the reasonable and customary fee.

Before your treatment, ask your provider to submit a pre-treatment review to the insurance company so that both you and the provider know up front what the insurance company will pay and what your cost will be for the procedure.

Avoid paying the difference in cost between what your provider charges and the reasonable and customary fee by asking your doctor to accept your insurance company's payment of the reasonable and customary fee as payment in full. If this tactic doesn't work, consider looking for another doctor who will accept this amount.

Major medical coverage

Major medical coverage, normally purchased along with basic coverage, supplements basic policy benefits by covering the major expenses of a catastrophic illness or injury. Major medical coverage comes into play when basic coverage benefit amounts are used up. After the insured pays the deductible (toward the amount for covered charges that basic coverage did not pay), major medical insurance may reimburse expenses for the greater portion of covered charges — the services that go beyond what a basic plan covers. These charges may include unpaid, covered hospital expenses such as

- Hospital room and board
- General nursing services
- Additional hospital services
- Surgeon's and physician's fees

- Anesthetics

- Anesthesiologists' services

- Charges incurred out of the hospital such as for home care for extended periods and prescriptions

Policies usually include a maximum level of benefits, too. The maximum amount the insurance company will pay for a particular service or over the lifetime of the policy is called a *cap*.

Most major medical coverage includes an annual *out-of-pocket maximum clause*. This provision limits the initial amount (deductible and coinsurance) that you must pay during a set period, usually a year. (Premiums aren't considered part of the out-of-pocket expenses.) After you pay this amount, the insurer pays 100 percent of all remaining, covered expenses that you incur during that period.

Understanding costs

Enrollees in a fee-for-service plan pay a monthly premium. After they meet the deductible, members share subsequent covered expenses with the insurance company. For example, assume that you have a $2,500 deductible. You pay the first $2,500 of covered expenses within a calendar year. You may then share the cost of the next covered expense you incur — perhaps the insurance company pays 80 percent of your next covered doctor visit, and you are responsible for the remaining 20 percent (your *coinsurance*).

To receive payment for fee-for-service claims, you most likely have to fill out claim forms and send them to your insurance company. Sometimes your doctor's staff fills out claim forms for you.

Keep receipts for all your medical expenses. Without receipts, you have no way of tracking whether the insurance company considered and appropriately reimbursed every expense you submitted. See Chapter 7 for information on keeping good records and coordination of benefits.

Keep your needs in mind and ask some of the following questions during your investigation of fee-for-service plans:

■ What is covered?

■ What are the limitations?

■ What is the total annual cost? The total annual deductible? The total annual coinsurance?

■ What is my maximum out-of-pocket expense?

■ What is the lifetime maximum the insurer will pay?

Table 1-1 lists the pros and cons of fee-for-service plans.

Table 1-1: Pros and Cons of Fee-for-Service Plans

Pros	Cons
Members can choose any doctor or hospital and can consult any specialist they choose.	May not cover certain preventive services, such as routine physicals, to the extent that HMOs and PPOs do.
	You must pay a deductible before receiving benefits.
	You must file your own claim forms.

Consider fee-for-service plans if you want to make your own health care choices, even though doing so is more expensive and involves more paperwork. Make sure that the plan you buy offers both basic and major medical coverage.

Managed Care Plans

Managed care is a way to control cost. It refers to the way in which health insurance plans monitor how much health care you use. For example, if you need to see a specialist, a plan may require a referral from your primary care doctor to assure that the consultation with the specialist is necessary.

All managed care plans require you to pay a monthly premium. You or your employer may pay the entire premium, or you may share the cost with your employer.

Health maintenance organization (HMO)

A health maintenance organization (HMO) is an insurance plan that provides health care by hospitals, doctors, and other medical professionals within a network. Plan members must use the providers within this network for the HMO to cover their medical expenses. In emergencies or when deemed medically necessary, HMOs may make exceptions and permit members to use providers outside of the network.

In almost all HMOs, you must have a primary care physician (PCP). Sometimes the plan assigns a PCP to you; sometimes you get to choose one. The responsibility of the primary care physician is to keep an eye on your health, provide most of your medical care, and refer you to specialists and other health care professionals when necessary.

If you see a specialist without a referral from your primary care physician, you may have to pay the specialist's bill yourself.

Many HMOs offer a *point-of-service (POS) plan,* which entitles members to refer themselves outside the plan and still get some coverage (an advantage to members who may need out-of-network specialists for certain medical conditions).

Not all HMOs offer the same services. Some plans may limit services such as outpatient mental health care. However, HMOs usually provide preventive care as a cost-saving measure. Because HMOs receive a fixed fee for your covered medical care, preventing serious, costly illness is in their interest.

Each time you use the services of the HMO, you pay either nothing or a small copayment, perhaps $5 or $10. You don't have to pay a deductible. Your total medical costs with an HMO are probably lower than with fee-for-service insurance.

Your paperwork is minimal in an HMO. By displaying your membership card at the time of service, you don't have to fill out claim forms for office visits or hospital stays.

During your research, talk with people who belong to the plan, and ask them about the plan's pros and cons. Additionally, ask the plan representative questions such as

- How large is the pool of primary care physicians I have to choose from?

- How difficult is changing primary care physicians and specialists? How often can I change primary care physicians?

- How far in advance do I have to make appointments with the doctor? Is this wait the same regardless of which doctor I use?

- What are the limitations on services?

- How do emergency services work?

- What do I do if I need treatment while I'm out of town or out of the country?

Think about the pluses and minuses of HMOs as you review Table 1-2.

Table 1-2:   Pros and Cons of HMOs

Pros	Cons
Always covers preventive care (physicals and immunizations).	You must use providers and hospitals within the network.
Has low out-of-pocket costs.	Your primary care physician must refer you to specialists.
Requires no claim forms.	You receive limited services, such as for mental conditions and substance abuse services.
No deductibles.	You may have to wait longer to get an appointment.

Preferred provider organization (PPO)

Preferred provider organizations (PPOs) combine features of traditional fee-for-service plans and HMOs. PPOs have contracts with doctors, hospitals, and other providers to accept lower fees from the insurer for their services. As with HMOs, members must use the network (preferred) providers for medical expenses to be fully covered.

With emergency care in some PPO plans, both the hospital and the attending physician must be in the network in order for the entire service to be considered in-network.

In a PPO, members can use (without a doctor's referral) doctors outside of the plan and still receive some coverage. This flexibility lets you keep your current doctor, even one who isn't part of the PPO's network.

In a PPO you pay more of the expenses than in an HMO and may have to fill out claim forms.

As with HMOs, some PPOs may expect you to choose a primary care physician to monitor your health care.

If you select a primary care physician who is not in the network, the cost is higher, which means that you have to meet a deductible and pay coinsurance based on those higher charges. You may also have to pay the difference between what the provider charges and what the plan pays.

PPOs usually cover preventive care. Your copayment is small when you see an in-network doctor, and you don't have to fill out any claim forms: Just present your membership card.

Carefully study the pros and cons of PPOs, listed in Table 1-3; they incorporate some features of both fee-for-service plans and HMOs.

Table 1-3:   Pros and Cons of PPOs

Pros	*Cons*
You sometimes receive coverage for preventive care.	You do have to fill out claim forms if you see a doctor outside the network.
Your out-of-pocket costs are lower within the network; you generally don't have to meet a deductible for in-network services.	You face higher out-of-pocket costs outside the network; you usually have to meet a deductible before the insurance company will consider their portion of the out-of-network claim.
You can use and refer yourself to doctors outside the network.	You have to deal with more paperwork for approvals. (Membersof PPOs usually need to obtain prior approval for inpatient care and certain outpatient procedures, whether or not the providers belong to the network.)
Your costs are paid as fee-for-service but at reduced cost.	May offer a range or only limited services.

Continuing Coverage

This section addresses what you can do to keep yourself covered — without a break in coverage — when you lose coverage under an employer's group insurance plan.

Definitions

First, some definitions:

- **Beneficiary:** Someone who is eligible to receive benefits under an insurance plan.

- **Medicare beneficiary:** The person — usually the patient — who is enrolled in the Medicare program (see Chapter 6) and receives the medical or other related services.

- **Qualified beneficiaries:** The spouse and/or dependent children covered under a group plan. If the plan is terminated, the employee is also considered a qualified beneficiary.

- **Qualifying event:** An event that normally would result in the loss of coverage under a group plan, such as when an employee dies, is laid off, is subject to reduced working hours, retires, or quits. A qualifying event may occur when a covered spouse divorces or separates from an employee, or when a child loses dependent status by turning a specified age (often 19 or higher; sometimes as high as 25 if a full-time student). A qualifying event triggers *continuation* or *conversion* rights.

- **Continuation:** Allows beneficiaries to continue coverage under the same group plan for a specified period.

- **Conversion:** Gives beneficiaries the opportunity to convert to individual or family coverage at individual or family rates.

Conversion options

By law, group plan administrators must give beneficiaries of a plan written notice of their rights to continue and convert coverage. They must do so when the employee's plan becomes effective, as well as when the plan changes to incorporate a new conversion option. Administrators must also give notice to beneficiaries within a specified number of days of a qualifying event (but the beneficiary — you — must notify the administrator that the qualifying event occurred). This notice should explain the deadline by which beneficiaries must tell the employer whether they plan to continue or convert coverage.

If you miss the deadline for notifying the employer of your intent to continue or convert coverage, you may lose your opportunity to do so.

Most plans require that an employee be enrolled in the group plan for at least three months before beneficiaries can exercise their continuation and/or conversion options. A covered spouse who divorces or separates from the employee and covered children no longer eligible for coverage under the employed parent's plan are the people most likely eligible for the conversion option. They don't need to submit proof of insurability, and pre-existing conditions — other than exclusions that already exist under the group plan — don't affect conversion, either.

Laws and provisions may vary. Always check your state's laws and your insurance policy, contract, and/or plan document for eligibility and other requirements governing continuation and conversion of coverage.

COBRA

Another kind of continued coverage is COBRA, a federal law under which certain workers and their families, previously enrolled in a group plan, may continue the same coverage with almost no change in premiums for a specified period. The Consolidated Omnibus Budget Reconciliation Act of 1985 (COBRA) requires certain companies, such as those with 20 or more employees, to offer health insurance coverage under COBRA. However, employers not subject to COBRA, such as certain church plans and some union-sponsored plans, often provide some conversion coverage, most likely with fewer benefits than those available under the group plan.

Coverage under COBRA allows eligible employees to keep the same coverage as under the group plan for 18, 29, or 36 months. A widowed or divorced spouse or a child who is no longer a dependent is also eligible. COBRA premiums are usually higher than under the group plan.

Warning

If an insurance carrier terminates a group plan, you can't continue your coverage or convert it to COBRA.

COBRA can furnish excellent short-term coverage, bridging the gap until you find a new job with health coverage or another policy elsewhere.

You have 60 days from the date of group coverage termination to decide whether to enroll in COBRA. If you choose to do so, the coverage effective date is retroactive to the date the group plan ended. You then have 45 days from the date you choose to enroll in CORBA to make your first premium payment. When your coverage under COBRA runs out, you may convert your plan as described in the previous section.

CHAPTER 2
MAKING SENSE OF COSTS

IN THIS CHAPTER

- Understanding premiums and how to keep them down
- Sharing medical expenses with your insurer
- Controlling what you spend on medical expenses
- Setting aside pretax dollars for health care expenses
- Thinking ahead with reasonable and customary fees

This chapter explains how your money is spent in a health insurance plan and shows you various ways to limit some of your health insurance costs.

Any reference in this book to charges that are applied to a deductible or reimbursed by an insurance plan pertain to *covered charges* only — expenses that are specifically included in your health insurance plan. Covered charges generally don't include expenses for nonmedical items related to an illness or injury or for items that the plan explicitly excludes. See your plan's policy, contract, and/or plan document for what your plan covers.

Paying for a Plan

A *premium* is what you or your employer pays on a monthly, biweekly, or quarterly basis for the coverage that a health insurance plan provides. The first premium you or your employer pays indicates that you accept the contract for health insurance coverage, and your coverage starts. The rest of your premiums keep the coverage in effect.

Your premium stays the same, whether you use the plan or not.

Insurance companies normally calculate group premiums a year at a time. Insurers increase or decrease premiums from time to time, basing the changes on how the group used a plan's services, as well as on related administrative costs incurred during a previous period.

When you're checking out an insurance plan, ask about any rate increases the plan imposed over the past five years and whether these increases applied to all of a company's plans or just to certain plans.

You can lower your premiums in several ways. One way is to accept a higher deductible. Another way is to carefully choose the length of your hospital *elimination period* (the number of days you have to be hospitalized before the plan pays benefits).

Large groups

Generally, the larger the group, the lower the cost. A large group contract means a higher volume of business to an insurer. Insurers can often administer contracts for large groups at a lower cost than contracts for individual policies because they can spread out the risk of providing coverage for one or more high-risk members. Insurance companies determine how much to charge for a group by looking at the claims experience of the entire group during an earlier period. They then charge an average, fixed premium for each group member for the next period of coverage.

Small groups

With fewer members, small groups have less ability to distribute risk. If the insurer covers a small group, the expense of carrying just one high-risk individual may outweigh the cost of carrying the remaining low-risk members. To protect themselves, insurers may charge higher premiums and limit coverage for the group.

Individual policies

Individual policy (usually a fee-for-service plan) premiums are often higher than a group policy because individuals don't have members among whom to spread the risk. Insurance companies calculate premiums for individual policies based on traits, such as overall health, occupation, gender, and age, of the applicant (and family members)

Table 2-1 shows a general, relative premium cost for various types of plans. Actual costs may vary greatly.

Table 2-1:   Relative Cost of Premiums

(Highest to Lowest)
COBRA (short-term coverage only)
Individual plan (fee-for-service)
Small group PPO
Small group HMO
Large group PPO
Large group HMO

Paying Your Part with Copayments

A *copayment* is a fixed dollar amount that you pay each time you use a medical service — perhaps $50 for a hospital visit, $25 for an emergency room treatment, or $5 or $10 for a doctor's visit. Health plans may also require copayments for prescriptions. The amounts of the copayments vary from plan to plan, so understanding what your plan charges is critical. (Some plans use the terms *copayment* and *coinsurance* interchangeably.)

Sharing Costs: Deductibles and Coinsurance

A *deductible* is the amount of covered charges you must pay before the plan begins to pay benefits. Expenses applied toward the deductible are eligible only if they are expenses that the plan covers. Typically, a new deductible starts over at the beginning of each calendar year.

Some plans impose a *per cause deductible,* where you must meet a separate deductible for each condition. Others have more than one deductible — one for general medical expenses, another for inpatient hospital expenses, and another for prescriptions.

Coinsurance is a fixed percentage that you pay after you pay the deductible. An *80/20 coinsurance rate,* for example, means that the insurance company pays 80 percent of the covered charges, and you pay 20 percent, after you've paid your deductible in full. HMOs usually don't have large deductibles or coinsurance.

Deductibles and coinsurance are a way to help keep the premiums for major medical policies affordable. Generally, premiums decrease as deductibles increase.

You can save money by keeping your deductible as large as possible, perhaps as high as the amount of medical costs you can afford in a year.

In a large family situation, health insurance plans may not require that every person meet his or her own deductible. Instead, health insurance plans usually require that only two or three family members must each meet a calendar-year deductible.

Usually members of a small family — two or three people — must each meet the entire individual deductible. Check for your own plan's specific provision.

Another alternative is a *family deductible,* or *aggregate maximum,* which is a way for a family to meet a deductible without each member having to meet the full deductible individually. Here's how it works: Suppose the plan's deductible is $500. One family member must meet the $500 deductible all by himself or herself. The insurance company begins to pay benefits for this person. After the first person meets the $500 deductible, you can combine the expenses of the remaining family members to meet a second $500 deductible. The insurance then begins to pays benefits for the rest of the family.

Limiting Expenses

Some insurance plans have provisions that limit the amount of money you pay for medical costs during the course of a year. Terminology for these provisions may vary from plan to plan, but you may see them called *cap, benefit limit, stop-loss, catastrophic limit,* or *maximum out-of-pocket.* Look for these provisions in the plans you consider. Be sure that you clearly understand how these provisions set your dollar limits, as well as the insurance company's dollar limits.

Maximum out-of-pocket

Out-of-pocket refers to the money that you, the insured, pay for deductibles and coinsurance. If you or a covered dependent has a serious illness or injury, hospital expenses can easily run into the thousands of dollars. One way insurance companies help you contain such potential costs is to limit your responsibility for them with an out-of-pocket maximum provision, sometimes referred to as a *stop-loss* provision or a *catastrophic limit.*

A maximum out-of-pocket provision sets a limit for the amount of your deductible plus coinsurance that you pay for a specific period — usually a year. After you reach this limit, the insurer pays 100 percent of the remaining covered charges during that period.

The lower your out-of-pocket limit, the higher the premium may be.

If you plan on purchasing family coverage, check your policy to make sure that it has an annual, aggregate, stop-loss amount.

You may face separate limits for both medical-surgical expenses and inpatient care for mental conditions.

Lifetime limit

Some health insurance policies set a *lifetime limit* for medical care expenses, which is the maximum amount an insurer will pay during the your lifetime. A good lifetime maximum is $5 million. Other plans have no lifetime limit.

As a rule, the higher the lifetime maximum, the better. As usual, you pay for this benefit increase through your premiums.

Using Pretax Dollars: FSAs

Employers may offer flexible spending accounts (FSAs; sometimes called *reimbursement accounts*) to their employees to help them save money. You set aside an established amount of money in an FSA, without paying taxes on it, and dedicate this amount for eligible medical expenses that health insurance plans don't cover. You can take advantage of this program even if you don't itemize deductions on your federal income tax return.

You must establish an FSA for a 12-month period. You can use the money in this account only for eligible expenses you incur during this 12-month period.

Money for these individual employee accounts comes from employee pretax contributions. Employees must contribute to the FSA throughout the entire 12-month period, although employees can make changes to their account if they experience an applicable life status change, as defined by the IRS, such as getting married or divorced, having a baby, or adopting a child.

Tip

Check with your employer to see whether a flexible spending account is available and what its regulations are, including what expenses are covered, as well as dependent eligibility, withdrawal deadlines, and reimbursement request requirements.

Flexible spending accounts come in two forms: health care and dependent care. (Dependent care accounts aren't directly related to health insurance, so this chapter doesn't discuss them in detail.) You must set them up as separate accounts. Only the specific type of care for which you create the account is eligible for reimbursement. You can use a health care FSA even if you don't get your health insurance through your employer. Check with your plan sponsor for the maximum amount you may set aside for each account.

To continue participating in a flexible spending account plan, you must enroll every year. Each time you enroll, you must let the plan sponsor know how much money you want to place in the account for the year. Sponsors may provide a worksheet like the one shown in Figure 2-1 to help you calculate this amount. Consider several kinds of health care expenses that your health insurance plan doesn't cover, such as annual deductibles, copayments and coinsurance, expenses for eyeglasses, orthodontic expenses, and routine physical exams.

Figure 2-1:   A sample FSA qualifying expense worksheet.

MEDICAL REIMBURSEMENT ACCOUNT
QUALIFYING EXPENSE WORKSHEET

QUALIFYING EXPENSE	ESTIMATED ANNUAL EXPENSE
Medical Expenses:	
Medical Doctor's Fees/Copayments	$_____
Annual Physical Examinations	$_____
Prescriptions	$_____
X Rays	$_____
Lab Fees	$_____
Hospital Services	$_____
Chiropractors	$_____
Surgery	$_____
Ambulance Service	$_____
Psychiatrists	$_____
Psychologists	$_____
Alternative treatments	$_____
Vision Expenses:	$_____
Eye Exams	$_____
Lenses/Frames	$_____
Contact Lenses	$_____
Dental Expenses:	$_____
Teeth Cleaning	$_____
Braces	$_____
Dentures, bridges, crowns, and so on	$_____
X Rays	$_____
Fillings	$_____
Hearing Expenses:	$_____
Exams	$_____
Hearing Aids	$_____
Other Eligible Expenses	$_____
TOTAL ANNUAL MEDICALLY RELATED EXPENSES	$_____
PER PAY PERIOD ELECTION (DIVIDE ANNUAL EXPENSES BY THE NUMBER OF PAY CHECKS PER YEAR)	$_____

You cannot obtain reimbursement for:

1. The basic cost of Medicare insurance (Medicare A).
2. Life insurance or income protection policies.
3. Accident or health insurance for you or members of your family.
4. The hospital insurance benefits tax withheld from your pay as part of the Social Security tax or paid as part of Social Security self-employment tax.
5. Illegal operations or drugs.
6. Travel your doctor told you to take for rest or change.
7. Cosmetic Surgery.

Health insurance plan premiums aren't eligible for reimbursement from an FSA. Check with your employer for other options for premiums.

The full dollar amount that you elect to place in your health care FSA for the 12-month period, minus any amounts you've already received as reimbursement, must be available to you at all times. Suppose that you decide to set up an FSA for $1,200. Your employer deposits $100 per month of your pretax salary to your account. You incur a medical expense in March — your first expense for the year — and you are responsible for paying $600. Even though $600 is more than the total deposited so far in your account, you are entitled to reimbursement because your annual amount will eventually be $1,200. If you want to claim expenses from a flexible spending account, your employer will probably require you to do the following:

1. Complete a claim form (request for reimbursement).

2. Attach all receipts from the medical service providers for eligible expenses.

3. Submit bills to your health care plan(s) first. After the insurance provider rejects the bills, you must submit the rejection notice and the bills with the claim form.

4. Include a written statement that the expenses aren't eligible for reimbursement from your health care plan(s). (The claim form may already include this statement for you to sign.)

5. Submit all the paperwork for reimbursement to the FSA administrator.

If you don't use all the money in your health care FSA by the end of the claim out period for the plan year, by law you will lose it. (But you don't pay taxes on the amount you don't receive.) The plan sponsor cannot return these funds to you. The funds can't carry over into next year's account, and they can't be used to pay for other benefits.

However, the plan sponsor can use these funds in a couple of different ways. For example, they can offset losses resulting from participants who requested their full reimbursement amount but terminated employment before they actually contributed the full amount to their FSAs.

For current Internal Revenue Service regulations on federal tax treatment of health insurance premiums and other related medical expenses, check www.irs.gov on the Web, contact your local IRS office, or use the following toll-free numbers: live telephone assistance: 800-829-1040; for people with hearing impairments: 800-829-4059 (TDD); Tele-Tax recorded tax information: 800-829-4477. Consult your local telephone directory for local numbers and other toll-free services.

Calculate what you think you'll need from your FSA during the coming year carefully. Consider electing an amount lower than what you think you'll need so that if your expenses are less than you expect, you don't lose your funds. Also be sure to submit all requests for reimbursement and the necessary paperwork by the deadline. If you don't, you risk forfeiting the remaining money in your FSA account for that year.

Reasonable and Customary Fees

Most health insurance plans set the portion of fees they will cover for specific services. They base these amounts on the fees that most providers normally charge for a particular service in the same geographic area. These established amounts are called *reasonable and customary (R&C) fees.* They may also be called *usual and customary (U&C); regional/reasonable and customary (R&C);* and *usual, customary, and regional/ reasonable (UCR).*

Here's an example: You plan on undergoing a surgical procedure for which your doctor charges $1,500. Most doctors in your geographic area charge $1,200. Because $1,200 is considered the reasonable and customary fee, the insurance company bases its coverage on $1,200. For your surgery, you pay the usual deductible and coinsurance, plus the $300 difference between what your doctor charges and the reasonable and customary fee.

You may not apply the difference between what your doctor charges and the reasonable and customary fee to your maximum out-of-pocket amount, even if you go beyond your stop-loss limit (see the section "Maximum out-of-pocket," earlier in this chapter). This amount is yours and only yours to pay.

You can try to avoid this extra cost by doing the following:

- Ask your doctor to accept whatever the insurance company pays as payment in full for the service.

- Look for a doctor whose fee is in line with the reasonable and customary fee.

- Request that the insurer review your claim in case of error or extenuating circumstances, such as an unrelated health condition that requires additional medical safeguards or procedures.

After a plan determines the reasonable and customary fee, it may pay on a percentage of this fee — rather than on the whole amount. Table 2-2 shows several examples of how insurers pay, based on a reasonable and customary fee of $1,000 for a surgical procedure, and what you end up paying. These examples assume that your portion of the coinsurance is 20 percent and that the insurance company's portion is 80 percent. Assume that you have already met the deductible.

Table 2-2: **Who Pays What**

Surgeon's Charge	% of R&C Fee Used as Basis for Figuring Coinsurance	Insurer Pays 80% Coinsurance	You Pay 20% Coinsurance	You Also Pay Difference between Surgeon's Charge and Sum of Coinsurances	Your Total Cost
$900	100% ($900)	$720 (80% of $900)	$180 (20% of $900)	$0	$180
$1,000 (= R&C)	100% ($1,000)	$800 (80% of $1,000)	$200 (20% of $1,000)	$0	$200
$1,200	100% ($1,000)	$800 (80% of $1,000)	$200 (20% of $1,000)	$200	$400
$900	80% ($720)	$576 (80% of $720)	$144 (20% of $720)	$180	$324
$1,000 (= R&C)	80% ($800)	$640 (80% of $800)	$160 (20% of $800)	$200	$360
$1,200	80% ($800)	$640 (80% of $800)	$160 (20% of $800)	$400	$560

CHAPTER 3
UNDERSTANDING MEDICAL COVERAGE

IN THIS CHAPTER

- Finding out about benefits for different types of services
- Avoiding surprises in coverage
- Legislating pre-existing conditions
- Considering an alternative path

The goal of this chapter is to help you avert surprises by making you aware of some of the nuances of plan benefits. Knowing ahead of time how a plan covers various medical expenses may influence some of your health care decisions. Changes in health care legislation may also affect your benefits.

Doctor Office Visits

When you check into how your health insurance plan covers doctor office visits, ask about the difference in coverage between routine visits, such as checkups and wellness services, and visits for illness or injury. Some plans may pay differently, depending on the reason for the visit and whether the provider is in or out of the plan network. Plans may require copayments, set annual limits for wellness services, or require that you meet a deductible before they pay anything.

Preventive Care

Preventive care covers a wide range of services, all intended to promote and maintain health. Preventive medicine may include the following:

- Blood pressure control
- Diet and exercise counseling
- Family counseling
- Immunizations for tuberculosis and influenza
- Mammograms and Pap smears
- Regular, routine physicals
- Risk management and substance abuse counseling, including education about the dangers of tobacco, alcohol, drug use, and high-risk sexual behaviors
- Screening for cancer, tuberculosis, cholesterol, and AIDS
- Well-baby checkups

When you have no symptoms, many traditional health insurance plans pay little or nothing for preventive care.

HMOs believe that detecting illness early may enhance the likelihood of appropriate and successful treatment. HMOs receive a fixed fee for covered medical expenses. They find that they save money in the long-term by paying for preventive care, which catches problems before they require expensive treatment. Covered services vary among HMOs, so as always, check the details of your plan.

Most PPOs also cover preventive care.

Maternity Care

Health insurance plans vary in the way they treat maternity and childbirth expenses. Some policies provide benefits for pregnancy complications but not for normal deliveries. Many policies won't pay for certain procedures, such as elective cesarean deliveries or abortions.

In some cases, you may need to add a *rider* (a document that changes provisions in the original policy) to your basic health insurance policy to get coverage for prenatal care, normal delivery services, and routine, newborn nursery care (at the hospital). Such a plan may have a separate lifetime maximum amount for normal maternity services.

Maternity riders are generally very expensive, with high premiums and low caps on coverage. For example, the cost of the rider may be equivalent to 40 percent of the cap. In addition, a maternity rider may provide no benefits the first year, 50 percent of the cap during the second year, and full coverage after that.

The Newborns' and Mothers' Health Protection Act of 1996 (NMHPA) sets the minimum number of days in the hospital after giving birth for which group health plans, insurance companies, and HMOs must provide coverage. This act applies only to those plans that already provide coverage for hospital stays related to childbirth. After a normal, vaginal delivery, most plans must generally provide coverage for at least 48 hours for both the mother and newborn child. Health coverage for a hospital stay after a cesarean delivery must generally be at least 96 hours for both the mother and newborn child. NMHPA's requirements affect health plans beginning on or after January 1, 1998.

Infertility Treatment

Whether your health insurance plan covers infertility treatment may depend on government regulations. State regulations governing infertility treatment apply to health insurance that you buy on your own and that your employer buys. ERISA governs employers' self-insured plans.

Government regulations

If the state you live in has an infertility insurance mandate, you are entitled to infertility coverage, especially if the mandate is a *hard mandate* or a *mandate to provide*, meaning that health insurance underwriters must *provide* coverage. A *mandate to offer* or *soft mandate* requires underwriters to *offer* coverage to employees. Employers aren't obligated to buy the coverage. Table 3-1 gives some examples of hard and soft mandates. See the Web site of the American Society for Reproductive Medicine, `www.asrm.com/patient/insur.html`, which lists the statutes for each state.

Table 3-1: Examples of Hard and Soft State Mandates

Hard Mandates	Soft Mandates
One cycle of in vitro fertilization after several conditions have been met	Coverage of infertility diagnosis and treatment, excluding in vitro fertilization but including gamete intrafallopian transfer (GIFT)
Comprehensive infertility diagnosis and treatment, including assisted reproductive-technology procedures	Coverage of comprehensive infertility diagnosis and treatment, including assisted reproductive-technology procedures
Infertility treatment as a preventive health care service benefit (HMOs)	Coverage of infertility diagnosis and treatment, including in vitro fertilization
Diagnosis and treatment of correctable medical conditions	

Some health insurance plans, such as the ones that churches and school districts buy, may also be exempt from state regulation.

ERISA (Employee Retirement Income Security Act) regulates employers' self-insured plans, which are exempt from state mandates. ERISA has no provision for infertility treatment.

Coverage

Some of the health insurance plans that cover infertility consider infertility a catastrophic event that affects worker productivity. Some plans that don't cover infertility may pay for infertility treatments that are permissible under other covered benefits, such as pelvic surgeries.

Unless your insurance plan contract specifically excludes infertility, you should be covered. If your contract does have an exclusion, read the contract carefully to understand what, specifically, is excluded.

Under the Americans with Disabilities Act (ADA), employers must treat persons with disabilities the same as they treat other employees with respect to the terms and conditions of employment, including fringe benefits such as health insurance coverage. The United States Supreme Court ruled that reproduction is a major life activity under the ADA. Therefore, infertility is a disability.

Title VII of the Civil Rights Act of 1964, as amended by the Pregnancy Discrimination Act (PDA), affirms that discrimination based on pregnancy, childbirth, or related medical conditions is considered sex discrimination. Because infertility is regarded as a medical condition related to pregnancy, employers must provide you with the same benefits such as insurance and time off from work as their other employees.

Medical Tests and X Rays

Some health insurance plans pay 100 percent of covered charges for routine and diagnostic medical tests and X rays, up to an annual dollar limit. For example, the plan may pay the first $100, after which you pay a deductible and coinsurance. With other plans, you may have to pay first: You pay the deductible and coinsurance, and then the plan pays 80 percent (for an in-network provider) or 50 percent (for an out-of-network provider) of the covered charges.

Comparing Accidents to Illnesses

If you run a high fever or fall out of a tree, you may visit a hospital emergency room. Both of these conditions is an "emergency" to your mind, and accordingly, you expect your health insurance plan to cover the associated charges, according to the *schedule of benefits,* a table or list showing the maximum amounts a plan pays for covered expenses.

However, some plans may pay one benefit for visits to the emergency room for an illness, such as a fever, and another benefit for an accident, such as falling from a tree. Other plans pay the same regardless of the reason for the visit.

Make sure that you clearly understand what your plan pays for a visit to the emergency room, whether for an illness or for an accident. Also check whether the plan requires notice before you visit the emergency room and, if so, what the penalty is for not giving notice.

Hospital Care

Health insurance plans may impose a deductible and coinsurance or a daily copayment amount for hospital coverage. In either case, the plans usually limit coverage to the rate for a *semi-private* hospital room, as defined in the insurance policy. Payment may differ based on whether the hospital is in a plan's network.

Check your hospital bill carefully: Mistakes are common. Make sure you actually received each service the bill lists.

Surgery (Inpatient and Outpatient)

The insurance industry defines *surgery* as

- A treatment that breaks the skin

- An examination that uses a scope that goes farther than the normal body opening

- Burn treatment

- Tissue removal

- Treatment of open and closed fractures

Coverage for surgeons' fees for surgical procedures may vary depending on whether the provider is in-network. These rates also apply to surgery-related services, such as anesthesiology, pathology, and radiology.

Find out ahead of time whether both the surgeon and the hospital are members of the plan network.

Some plans pay 100 percent of fees for outpatient surgery, which is probably less expensive than inpatient surgery because you spend your recovery period at home instead of in the hospital.

You may pay a penalty if you don't get *certification* (advance authorization) before you enter the hospital or before you undergo outpatient surgery. Check your plan's provisions.

Insurers usually base their coverage on reasonable and customary fees (see Chapter 2) for surgical procedures.

Pre-Existing Conditions

The term *pre-existing condition* used to refer to a health condition that was diagnosed or treated during a certain time before the date an insurance policy took effect, or for which a prudent person would have sought treatment. This definition gave insurers a fair amount of leeway in imposing exclusions and waiting periods for pre-existing conditions.

The definition of "pre-existing condition" — and regulations based on that definition — changed with the Health Insurance Portability and Accountability Act (HIPAA). This section explains how HIPAA may benefit insured persons who have pre-existing conditions.

Individual states may set their own, stricter obligations on insurers in certain areas, such as shortening the maximum waiting periods and requiring special enrollment periods. Check with your state's insurance department for these changes. (To find information on your state insurance department, contact the National Association of Insurance Commissioners, listed in the Resource Center.)

Health Insurance Portability and Accountability Act (HIPAA)

HIPAA defines "pre-existing condition" as "a condition (whether physical or mental) regardless of the cause of the condition, for which medical advice, diagnosis, care, or treatment was recommended or received." The definition no longer includes a condition for which a prudent person would have sought treatment.

Health insurers used to have the option to deny a new plan member's coverage of a pre-existing condition until after a waiting period. They could even refuse coverage for a person with a poor health history or with a specific illness, such as cancer or AIDS.

The HIPAA, which took effect July 1, 1997, changed this situation. All group health plans with two or more participants are subject to this law, whose main purpose is to make health coverage more continuous and more portable for people who change jobs, especially for people who have a pre-existing condition. The following descriptions and explanations are some of the highlights of HIPAA.

Prohibiting discrimination

Insurers can't deny coverage to eligible employees and their dependents under a group health care plan or insurance policy based on their health condition, medical history, or other *evidence of insurability* (a statement of proof of a person's health condition or other health-related information). In addition, insurers may not charge employees higher premiums or plan contributions based on these conditions.

Setting limits for exclusions

Under HIPAA, an insurer may apply a pre-existing condition exclusion or waiting period only if it's for a condition for which medical advice, diagnosis, care, or treatment was recommended or received during the six-month period before your enrollment date. (If you had a medical condition and didn't receive medical advice, diagnosis, care, or treatment within the six months before your enrollment date, then the condition is not considered to be pre-existing.) An insurer can apply a maximum waiting period of 12 months after your enrollment date.

For example, if you received treatment for asthma in October and plan to enroll in a new policy the following January, the asthma may be considered a pre-existing condition and may be subject to, at most, a 12-month waiting period. (Until the waiting period is over, you pay the medical costs for treating the asthma.)

The waiting period must be reduced by the number of days the individual had previous *creditable coverage* — coverage under a group health plan (including COBRA; see Chapter 1),

HMO, individual health insurance policy, Medicaid, or Medicare — without any break in coverage of more than 62 days. Coverage made up only of *excepted benefits* — benefits provided under a separate policy — such as coverage solely for dental or vision benefits, doesn't count.

So, for example, if you have seven months of creditable coverage, the new plan may impose a five-month waiting period for a pre-existing condition. However, if a previous health plan covered you continuously for five months, and then COBRA covered you for seven months, you receive credit for 12 months of coverage by your new group health plan and avoid a waiting period altogether.

The maximum waiting period differs for late enrollees: 18 months is the maximum waiting period allowed for conditions treated within the six months before enrollment. A *late enrollee,* or entrant, is a plan member or dependent who enrolls in a plan on a date other than

- The earliest date on which coverage can become effective under the terms of the plan

- On a special enrollment date, such as when a change in family status occurs or you experience loss of group coverage under another plan

Employees or dependent spouses who are otherwise eligible but not enrolled in a plan aren't considered late enrollees if they enroll in a group plan within 30 days of one of the following:

- A loss of eligibility for group coverage under another plan due to separation, divorce, death, termination of employment, reduction in work hours, termination of employer contribution toward coverage, termination of COBRA, or state-mandated continuation of coverage

■ A change in family status due to marriage, birth of a child, or adoption of a child

Some of the new limits set by HIPAA disallow exclusions for newborns, for children adopted while the employee is covered under the plan, and for pregnancy (including late enrollees).

Guaranteeing availability and renewability

An applicant may receive credit *(creditable coverage)* for previous health insurance as long as the coverage didn't lapse more than 62 days. Group health plans and health insurance issuers are required to provide a certificate of coverage, showing the dates that an individual is covered by a group health plan, to document their creditable coverage. By showing this certificate to the new group plan administrator, you can get credit toward a pre-existing exclusion period.

Special enrollment rights permit individuals to enroll without having to wait until the plan's next regular enrollment period. These rights are provided to employees who were eligible for and declined enrollment in the plan when first offered because they were covered under another plan, and to individuals upon marriage or upon the birth or adoption of a new dependent.

Providing better access to individual coverage

If you left a job that provided group health insurance coverage or had coverage under another plan for more than 18 months without a break of more than 62 days, HIPAA makes getting individual insurance (or satisfying a group plan's pre-existing condition clause) easier for you.

Individuals must meet the following requirements to be eligible for access to individual insurance:

- You must have been covered for at least 18 months, most recently under a group health plan

- Your group coverage wasn't terminated because of fraud on the individual's part

- You aren't eligible for or have exhausted your COBRA (or similar state provision) benefits

- You aren't eligible for coverage under another group health plan, Medicare or Medicaid, or any other health insurance coverage

If you haven't had group coverage and are having difficulty getting insurance on your own, check with your state insurance department to see whether your state has a high-risk health insurance pool.

Don't try to avoid a waiting period by hiding a condition. Insurance companies investigate thoroughly, and they will catch you.

Certifying a Medical Procedure

A health insurance policy often includes a *pre-admission certification* provision. Before you enter the hospital as an inpatient for (non-emergency) surgery or other type of service, you must apply for *pre-certification* — advance authorization for the hospital stay. Pre-admission certification allows a health insurance plan to determine whether a proposed treatment or service is medically necessary, whether it is covered by the plan, and how long the hospital stay should be, based on established medical criteria. Certification helps a plan limit its costs by weeding out unnecessary procedures and services. Without this certification, a policy may not cover your hospital stay.

With some health insurance plans, you, your doctor or hospital, or another health care provider must notify the plan in writing or by telephone before the date of treatment or service, usually within 72 hours. Expect to provide details such as the following:

■ Diagnosis

■ Related symptoms and their duration

■ Results of any physical exam, lab tests, and X rays

■ Treatment plan

■ Doctor and facility information

■ Proposed admission date and number of inpatient days required

■ Date of proposed surgery or other procedure

The plan subsequently notifies you of its decision. If certain treatments or services aren't certified, the insurer may reduce benefits by a penalty (see the schedule of benefits).

Warning

If you go to the hospital for an emergency, you may still have to notify your health insurer within a specified time to avoid a penalty.

Alternative Care

In recent years, the dollar amount that Americans spend on alternative treatments (also referred to as *nontraditional, unconventional,* and *complementary* treatments), herbs, vitamins, and supplements has gone up dramatically. Little by little, health insurance plans have begun to cover some of the following alternative treatments:

■ **Acupuncture**

■ **Biofeedback**

- **Chiropractic**
- **Homeopathy**
- **Massage therapy**

The insurer may put a cap on what it pays for each treatment, or it may limit the number of treatments it covers per year. Some health insurance plans may also impose certain restrictions, such as paying only when you use a network provider.

CHAPTER 4
UNDERSTANDING DENTAL AND VISION COVERAGE

IN THIS CHAPTER

- Understanding dental insurance options
- Checking out the benefits in dental insurance plans
- Looking into insurance coverage of vision care

Taking care of your teeth is as important as taking care of the rest of your health. If you visit the dentist regularly, you're more likely to catch disease in its early stages and avoid expensive treatments, making the cost of dental care much less than medical care.

Dental insurance plans encourage patients to get regular preventive care. This chapter looks at insurance coverage for various aspects of preventive care as well as coverage for treatment of dental conditions.

Preventing eye disease is just as important to your total health picture as dental care is. Vision care coverage encourages you to take preventive measures, such as having regular eye examinations, to keep your eyes healthy and diagnose problems at an early stage. This chapter closes with examples of what vision care plans may offer.

Dental Care

Although many health insurance plans exclude dental care, some plans may cover routine office visits or *orthodontia* (straightening of the teeth). When a plan doesn't cover dental care, it may offer an option to buy separate dental insurance to add to your health insurance policy. Dental insurance plans may use a network of dental care providers, similar to health care networks.

To control costs, a dental insurance plan may impose a dollar limit *(cap)* on the amount of benefits the plan pays. Plans may also restrict — or even exclude — the number and/or types of services that are covered to keep costs down.

Dental care coverage varies and may include the following:

- Crowns and bridges

- Endodontics (root tips, nerves)

- Oral surgery, periodontics (gums, bone)

- Orthodontia (braces)

- Prosthetics (bridges, dentures, partials)

- Restorative services, such as fillings

- Routine diagnostic and preventive services, such as examinations, X rays, and cleaning

If you use dentists within a network of dental care providers, you may receive full coverage for routine exams and cleanings, and you may pay lower prices for other treatments. Dental networks usually require you to file a claim.

Another way to control costs is with a dental discount card program, which is often offered in conjunction with — but separately from — your health insurance plan. Dentists who participate in a dental discount card network provide discounts on several of the most common dental services such as examinations, fillings, and gum treatments. If you're a member of a dental discount card program, just show your card each time you visit the dentist.

Cleaning and X rays

Dentists use *prophylaxis* (teeth cleaning) and X rays to diagnose oral health conditions. Dental insurance plans may cover only a limited number of these services per year.

If you choose a dental insurance plan that uses deductibles and coinsurance (as opposed to the discounts that a dental discount card program provides), look for a plan that covers diagnostic and preventive services, such as those shown in Table 4-1, at 100 percent.

Table 4-1:   Dental Diagnostic and Preventive Services

Service	Frequency
Initial oral examination	Once per dentist
Teeth cleaning	Twice per year
Complete X rays	Once every three years
Bitewing X rays (crowns of top and bottom molars to show decay between teeth and under fillings)	Once per year
Fluoride treatment	Twice per year

Routine restorative care

Routine restorative care is a fancy way to refer to dental fillings. Check to see what types of services your plan considers routine restorative care and what benefits the plan pays for these services. In the examples in Table 4-2, Plan 1 covers 80 percent of restorative treatment, and Plan 2 covers 100 percent.

Oral surgery and orthodontia

Oral surgery embodies a variety of procedures, including the following:

- Endodontics (treating root canals for diseases of the pulp and bone, removing tooth nerves, bleaching discolored teeth, managing traumatic injuries to the teeth, and performing related surgery to help preserve the natural teeth in a healthy state)

- Periodontics (treating complicated periodontal disease involving bone grafts or underlying tissues)

- Placing or restoring dental implants

- Removing impacted teeth, tissue biopsy, and draining minor oral infections

Because many dental insurance plans emphasize and encourage preventive care, some plans may pay only 50 percent of expenses for oral surgery. Other plans, as Table 4-2 shows, may pay 80 to 100 percent. Examine your plan in detail to learn what the oral surgery benefits are.

Orthodontia involves straightening teeth and treating problems related to the growth and development of the jaws. The sample plans in Table 4-2 cover orthodontia at 50 percent, with no deductible, and impose a $1,000 lifetime maximum.

Treatments for temporomandibular joint (TMJ) syndrome, which affects the joints at the jaw, is usually covered under medical, rather than dental, insurance.

Your dental insurance plan may pay benefits for oral surgery and/or orthodontia procedures based on reasonable and customary fees.

Some insurers may write plans to include a separate deductible for dental care and an annual maximum on payments. You may have a waiting period after the policy takes effect for some major dental procedures.

If your plan has a provision that sets an annual maximum benefit for dental care, think about dividing up and receiving treatment over several years, if feasible. Watch for lifetime maximums on certain types of dental care, such as orthodontia.

Table 4-2 shows two examples of dental coverage in a dental insurance plan. Plan 2 has lower deductibles and a higher annual maximum benefit than in Plan 1, but Plan 2 restricts its members to using services from providers within the network.

Table 4-2:   Examples of Dental Coverage

	Plan 1	*Plan 2*
Annual deductible	$50 per person, $150 per family	$25 per person, $75 per family
Annual maximum benefit	$1,750 per person	$2,500 per person
Diagnostic, teeth cleaning, X rays, fluoride treatment	Covered at 90 to 100% if patient uses PPO dentist. No deductible.	Covered at 100%. No deductible.

The following percentages of coverage are payable after the patient meets the deductible.

Restorative treatment	Covered at 80%	Covered at 100%
Crowns and caps	Covered at 50%	Covered at 80%
Oral surgery (simple and surgical extractions, excluding impacted teeth)	Covered at 80%	Covered at 100%

Continued

Table 4-2: **Examples of Dental Coverage**
(continued)

	Plan 1	Plan 2
Other oral surgery (including impacted teeth)	Covered at 80%	Covered at 50%
Endodontics/ apicoectomy (removal of root abscess), root canal	Covered at 80%	Covered at 80%
Periodontics	Covered at 80%	Covered at 80%
Mouth-prop devices, space maintainers, and sealants	Covered at 80%	Covered at 100%
Prosthodontics (replacement of missing teeth)	Covered at 50%	Covered at 50%
Crowns when inserted to affix bridges	Covered at 50%	Covered at 50%
Orthodontia	Covered at 50%, $1,000 lifetime maximum benefit	$1,000 lifetime maximum benefits. No deductible.

Vision Care

Coverage for vision care through employer-sponsored health insurance plans may vary widely. Vision care plans most often cover examinations, lenses, and frames on a scheduled basis, paying a fixed dollar amount for each benefit and perhaps discounted fees for eyeglasses and contact lenses. Some plans spell out the procedures and services that they exclude, such as the following:

■ Corneal modulation (changing the shape of the cornea through surgery or with corrective contact lenses)

- Eye exams for corrective lenses, including contact lenses, eyeglasses, and their fitting

- Radial keratotomy (a surgical procedure to correct near-sightedness)

- Refractive keratoplasty (corneal grafting)

A group health insurance plan may not provide vision care coverage at all, in which case you may opt to buy separate vision care insurance to add to your health insurance policy. A separate vision care insurance plan may use a network of vision care providers, similar to the networks in health insurance and dental insurance plans.

The major medical part of a health insurance plan, rather than a vision care plan, most likely covers eye surgery.

Vision care plans may establish a percentage or a flat fee for eye exams and limit the frequency of the exams (such as once every 12 or 24 months). For example, a plan may pay 100 percent of the cost for a vision exam if you use a provider within a network, and up to $40 for an out-of-network provider. Depending on the premium you want to pay, you may be able to choose a deductible amount, such as $10 or $25: The higher the deductible, the lower the premium.

In some cases, you may have to use providers within your plan's network to be eligible to receive coverage for eye-care services. If you need additional care, your plan may require a referral from a specific provider, such as your primary care physician, or ophthalmologist.

CHAPTER 5
GETTING COVERAGE FOR EXTRAORDINARY CIRCUMSTANCES

IN THIS CHAPTER

- Finding coverage for critical illness
- Taking a look at long-term care
- Thinking ahead about disability

This chapter helps prepare you *before* an accident, the onset of serious illness, or other critical health-related situations may occur by explaining the main points about types of insurance coverage that you can choose to meet your particular health insurance needs. Having this knowledge in advance can lessen the impact of a sudden change in health status.

Dread Disease Insurance

You may live in an area with a high incidence of a particular disease or condition. Perhaps family history raises concerns about your susceptibility to a critical illness or disease. In these situations, you may want to consider setting up a financial cushion — beyond what your health insurance policy offers — in anticipation of above-average medical expenses.

Some insurance companies offer specified or *dread disease* policies, most commonly cancer insurance. These policies pay a cash benefit for procedures and treatments that conventional medical insurance may not cover. The dread disease plans pay a fixed dollar amount for every day you're in the hospital or receive treatment on an outpatient basis only if you contract the specific disease or group of diseases that the policy cites.

Don't think of a dread disease policy as a replacement for general medical coverage: The policy may limit the amount of benefits it pays. In fact, some states regard dread disease policies as offering little value or protection to the policyholder and have banned or restricted such policies. The cost of a dread disease policy may not be very high because it covers very specific conditions. Even so, weigh the cost of the policy carefully compared to the benefits it pays before you buy.

Shopping for a plan

Think about your family history and lifestyle as you shop for a dread disease policy: These factors may help you get a sense of whether you're at risk for a particular disease. Start by examining plans carefully, because they often exclude coverage for problems resulting from the specified disease itself, such as infections, diabetes, and pneumonia. In some cases, you have to wait several years after you buy a policy before the plan will pay for treatments. Always check the fine print for the following:

- **All-inclusiveness:** Benefits should include expenses for items such as hospital stays, medicine, surgery, doctors' visits, radiation treatment, chemotherapy, and reconstructive surgery after a mastectomy.

- **Additional benefits during a hospital stay:** You may find a policy that offers additional benefits after you've been in the hospital for more than 90 days. Be warned, however, that research states that the average hospital stay for cancer is only 13 days.

- **Travel expenses:** When treatments mean traveling long distances to a hospital, you definitely want a policy that covers your travel expenses — and perhaps travel expenses for a companion.

■ **Double coverage pay:** Keep an eye out for whether the dread disease insurance plan will pay benefits even though you're covered under another policy. Also check whether the other policy will pay benefits if you have a dread disease policy. (See Chapter 7 for information on coordination of benefits.)

Most dread disease insurance policies exclude people who have already been diagnosed with the disease.

Experimental procedures

Insurance companies often pay for bone marrow transplants and stem cell transplants to treat leukemia and lymphoma. However, insurers may not pay for these types of transplants when they're used to treat other types of cancer, where they're still considered experimental.

When you're evaluating a dread disease insurance plan, ask about how the plan pays for experimental procedures.

Paying the price

Some dread disease insurance plans do one or more of the following:

■ Adjust premium payments based on your lifestyle or family history

■ Pay an initial lump sum and then pay for various costs

■ Pay a single lump sum at the time of initial diagnosis and then end the coverage (which helps to lower their premiums)

■ Increase premiums as you age

Critical illness insurance

People are living longer, so they're more apt to experience serious illnesses or injuries that can temporarily put them out of commission. A critical illness plan covers more than just one condition. When you don't need disability insurance (because you expect to be back on your feet), critical illness insurance steps in to fill the void.

In general, although benefits vary from plan to plan, critical illness insurance pays you a lump-sum benefit if you suffer one of the covered critical illnesses or injuries.

Catastrophic Coverage and Long-Term Care

Catastrophic limit is another way to refer to maximum out-of-pocket. In fact, major medical insurance is sometimes called *catastrophic insurance.* Major medical insurance may pay over an extended period for hospitalization costs and other health services that exceed the maximums your basic plan provides. See Chapter 1 for more information on major medical insurance.

Most insurance plans, whether public or private, don't cover home health care at all. If they do, the services they cover may be very limited. Some plans, for example, won't pay for a care provider who is a member of the immediate family.

One way to enhance coverage for catastrophic illness is to purchase a *catastrophic coverage policy.* These policies are designed to pay for hospital and medical expenses that exceed a very high deductible, perhaps $20,000 or more. Such policies may also provide for a fairly high maximum lifetime limit.

Another approach is to add a *living insurance rider* to a life insurance policy. A living insurance rider provides benefits to the insured — while the insured is still living — in case of a catastrophic illness.

Long-term care insurance policies are special policies that provide coverage for nursing home stays and home health care for a period established when you buy your policy. These policies are also called *convalescent care* or *nursing home insurance.* The policies are usually indemnity-type policies, meaning that they pay an established amount for each day of coverage you spend in a nursing home, regardless of the actual cost you incur.

Home health care

The goal of home health care can be to maintain, improve, or restore a person's health. Usually, a doctor orders home health care and writes a *plan of care,* or instructions for the patient and the caretakers. In addition to registered nurses and licensed practical nurses, many other kinds of care providers may play a role, including the following:

■ Home health aides and visiting nurses

■ Homemakers from an outside service (housekeeping duties; no medical-related duties)

■ Nutritionists

■ Personal care attendants (PCAs — meal preparation, bathing, laundry, light housekeeping, and so on)

■ Physical, speech, and occupational therapists

■ Social workers

Patients may also need certain pieces of equipment at home, such as hospital beds and accessories, respirators and oxygen tanks, wheelchairs, and walkers. Major medical policies usually cover these expenses.

Nursing home care

Nursing homes are characterized by the type of services they provide:

- **Custodial care homes:** These facilities are intended to maintain and support the individual's current level of health, while trying to prevent any further decline. People in custodial care homes usually need a place to live and help with activities of daily living, which non-medically trained professionals can provide. This type of nursing home is the lowest level and least expensive of the three.

- **Intermediate care facilities:** These facilities provide planned, continuous programs of nursing care for residents who can't live alone. These programs are preventive and rehabilitative.

- **Skilled nursing facilities (SNFs):** A doctor must prescribe care for people in these facilities. Registered nurses and other medical personnel provide specialized medical care 24 hours a day.

Major medical coverage may cover the cost of a skilled nursing facility, but not the cost of a custodial care facility.

See the Medicare and Medicaid sections in Chapter 6 for more information about catastrophic coverage and long-term care.

Disability

Beyond the challenges of suffering pain or discomfort and undergoing treatment, disability may also mean loss of income. To replace this loss, you may be able to draw on various sources of financial compensation, such as the following:

- **Social Security:** For those who are severely disabled and unable to work at all

- **Workers' compensation:** For work-related illness or injury

- **Civil service disability:** For federal and state government workers

- **Automobile insurance:** For disability due to an automobile accident

Check with your state insurance department to see whether your state mandates and monitors disability plans. In states that do, your employer automatically deducts premiums from your paycheck. You file claims directly with the state.

If you aren't eligible for one of these sources, you probably won't receive compensation for lost income (other than sick-leave benefits from your employer), which is where disability insurance comes in.

Short-term disability (STD)

Short-term disability insurance covers only loss from illness or disease; it excludes loss from accident or injury. Employer-sponsored plans may include STD insurance as part of a health insurance plan. Benefits generally pay a certain percentage of your salary for a certain number of weeks, based on your years of employment.

For short-term disability, experts advise that you not rely on disability insurance — the cost of an STD policy may outweigh the benefits. In addition to any sick-leave benefits your employer pays, live on your savings or the sale of an investment for a couple of months.

Long-term disability (LTD)

Long-term disability insurance kicks in when short-term disability ends, usually after 52 weeks. Its goal is to lessen the threat of financial disaster. LTD plans pay monthly benefits —

from periods of one year up to a lifetime, depending on your plan — when disability prevents you from returning to work. Your plan also specifies when your benefits begin, how much you will receive, and any coverage limitations.

Check with your employer to see whether a group long-term disability policy is available. Some LTD plans offered through employers may be more cost-effective than in individual plans.

Disability insurance replaces only a percentage of your lost wages, usually about 60 percent of your income *at the time you buy the plan.* This insurance doesn't cover the cost of rehabilitation, which is a medical expense. Medicare benefits (see Chapter 7), which cover medical expenses, take effect in your 25th month of disability.

Deciding whether to buy disability insurance depends on your individual situation. You need to consider several factors, including the following:

■ How much financial risk are you willing to assume if you're unable to work for an extended period?

■ How long can you live on your savings and investments?

■ What will it take, in terms of time and effort, to rebuild your savings and investments and recoup lost interest?

■ Can your spouse's income can make up for your lost wages?

If you decide to buy a disability insurance policy, think about the following:

■ **How the insurer defines "disability":** One insurer may define "disability" as being unable to perform the duties of your customary occupation. Another insurer's definition may mean that you can engage in no gainful employment at all.

- **When benefits begin:** Benefits may begin from one to six months or more after the start of disability. If you can afford the lost income, lower your premiums by choosing a later starting date.

- **Whether the policy covers both accident and illness.**

Remember

Benefits may be taxable depending on who pays the premiums for the disability policy. The following parameters usually hold true, but you should consult your tax professional with any questions:

- If you pay the premiums for an individual policy, the benefits you receive aren't subject to income tax.

- If your employer pays some or all of the premiums under a group policy, some or all of the benefits may be taxable.

CHAPTER 6
GETTING SUPPLEMENTAL COVERAGE

IN THIS CHAPTER

- Understanding benefit options for prescription drugs
- Finding out about mental health coverage
- Bridging the gap with short-term insurance
- Getting the picture on Medicare and Medicaid fundamentals
- Supporting children's health insurance programs

This chapter gives you a look at several types of supplemental health insurance — prescription drug programs, mental health coverage, short-term coverage, Medicare, Medicaid, and CHIP.

Prescription Drugs

As the cost of prescription drugs continues to rise, health insurance companies put much effort into finding ways to keep these costs in check. This section describes three practices that work toward accomplishing the goal of minimizing drug expenses.

Formularies

Insurers save money with prescription drug formularies. A *formulary* is a list of drugs that the health insurance plan approves. In a *closed formulary,* the insurer pays only for certain, approved drugs. If the drug you need isn't on the approved list, you pay the entire cost. An *open formulary* offers most drugs, but the prices of the drugs vary.

More and more, HMOs are using a three-stage format to set prices for prescription drugs. For example, you pay a copayment of $5 for a generic (no brand name) drug, $10 to $15 for a brand-name drug in the formulary, and around $30 for a brand-name drug outside the formulary.

If your plan has a closed formulary, and that formulary doesn't include your drug, check your plan carefully: It may have a provision that lets you request approval for benefit coverage of your drug.

Step therapy

Health insurance plans also limit the high cost of drugs through *step therapy.* Step therapy requires plan members to follow a specific progression of prescriptions. You start with the least-expensive medication and then move one prescription at a time toward the most expensive prescription, stopping when your condition is under control.

If you already know which prescription drug is successful for you, take action before you join a new plan. Call the new plan's member services department to see whether it restricts the drug you're taking. If the plan puts your medication in the Step 3 category, explain that you already take this medication. Ask whether you can leave out Steps 1 and 2. If the insurer denies your request, look for another plan.

Prescription drug card program

Your health insurance plan may offer a prescription drug card program. Prescription drug card programs are a way to give members discounts on prescription drugs when they fill their prescriptions at a pharmacy that is a member of a pharmacy network. You also save money when you get an FDA (Food and Drug Administration) approved, generic equivalent drug instead of the brand-name drug.

If you go outside the pharmacy network to purchase a generic or brand-name prescription, you pay the deductible and coinsurance. The plan pays only the amount it would pay if you bought the medication at a member pharmacy.

Mental Health Care

Mental illnesses are brain disorders that frequently make coping with life's daily tasks difficult. Mental illnesses may affect thinking, emotions, moods, and a person's ability to relate to other people.

Many health insurance plans provide some mental health coverage for psychological services that mental health practitioners, such as psychiatrists and licensed clinical social workers, provide. Coverage varies greatly from plan to plan. Some plans offer a fixed dollar amount for mental health services for each day of a hospital stay and limit the number of days covered. For outpatient services, plans may pay a fixed amount for each visit and limit the number of visits they cover for each year. With just a few examples, Table 6-1 shows how widely mental health insurance coverage can vary.

Table 6-1:   Examples of Mental Health Insurance Coverage in Three HMOs

	HMO 1	HMO 2	HMO 3
Inpatient services	Covered at 100%. Limit of 45 days per year.	$50 per day. Limit of 15 days per year. No lifetime maximum.	$240 per admission. Limit of 30 days per year. Detoxification days do not count toward inpatient rehabilitation days.

Continued

Table 6-1:   Examples of Mental Health Insurance Coverage in Three HMOs (continued)

	HMO 1	HMO 2	HMO 3
Outpatient services	$20 (individual) or $10 (group) per visit. Limit of 20 visits per year.	$20 (individual) or $10 (group) per visit. Limit of 30 visits per year. No lifetime maximum.	$10 per visit. Limit of 60 visits per year.

The Mental Health Parity Act (MHPA) of 1996 went into effect in January 1998. This law requires that the annual and lifetime benefit limits for mental illnesses be equal to the annual and lifetime benefit limits that health insurance plans offer for other illnesses and injuries. The requirements of this act don't apply to employers with fewer than 51 employees or to a group health plan whose costs increase 1 percent or more as a result of implementing MHPA's requirements.

Some states have passed their own, stricter parity (equality) laws for mental health coverage. The Consumer Insurance Guide, www.insure.com/health, describes each state's mental illness parity laws.

Hospital Indemnity Insurance

Hospital indemnity insurance pays a specified daily, weekly, or monthly amount to an insured person during a hospital stay. You choose the amount of coverage when you buy the plan, so the money you receive isn't based on the actual cost of the hospitalization. You can spend the amount you receive in any way you choose.

Some policies have an *elimination period* provision that pays benefits only after you've been in the hospital for a specific number of days. You can reduce your premiums by choosing a longer elimination period, but remember that hospitalizations are usually for relatively brief periods.

Short-Term Health Plans

Short-term insurance plans are designed to provide coverage for hospitalization and/or medical services for individuals and families when you find yourself temporarily out of health insurance.

Short-term policies do not cover pre-existing conditions.

With short-term policies, you get to choose the length of the policy. In many cases, coverage can begin immediately after you apply. Short-term plans are not renewable, but you can reapply for a second policy. However, the second coverage won't continue the coverage you had under the first plan; the second plan is brand-new. Consequently, the second plan considers any condition that occurred while you were covered under the first plan to be a pre-existing condition and doesn't cover it. The combined total coverage of both the first and second short-term policies usually can't exceed 365 days.

Eligibility requirements for short-term health insurance vary from plan to plan, so check the requirements of the plan you're considering carefully.

Short-term plans for students are specially designed to remain in effect during a student's full-time enrollment in an accredited college or university. Short-term health insurance policies are available in most states. For information on student plans, call your school or an insurance company or agent. For student and short-term plans in general, check with your state's insurance department for companies that sell short-term plans.

Medicare

The Health Care Financing Administration (HCFA) of the U.S. Department of Health and Human Services administers Medicare, the nation's largest health insurance program. Medicare (Title XVIII of the Social Security Act) covers people who are 65 years and older and are citizens or permanent residents of the United States, certain people who are disabled, and people with End-Stage Renal Disease.

Remember

If you reach the age of 65 and are still working, you may end up with health insurance through Medicare as well as through your employer-sponsored health plan. In this case, your employer-sponsored group health plan is the primary insurer (pays first) and Medicare is the secondary insurer (pays after the primary insurer pays). See Chapter 7 for more about primary and secondary insurers and coordination of benefits.

Dialing for details

HCFA, which administers Medicaid as well as Medicare, provides toll-free telephone numbers for information about your health plan benefits, rights, and options. It also provides information on the quality of managed care plans, Medigap insurance, and the Medicare + Choice program. (Later, this chapter discusses these programs in more detail.)

Call 800-MEDICARE, or 800-633-4227 (877-486-2048 if you have a TDD or TTY) 8:00 a.m. to 4:30 p.m., local time, weekdays. Talk to a customer service representative in English or Spanish for

- General information about Medicare and Medigap insurance

- General information about Medicare health plan options in your community

- Specific quality and satisfaction information about managed care plans

- Telephone numbers for help with billing questions about Medicare claims or other issues

After hours, use the automated options to

- Order *Medicare & You* handbooks or audiotapes in English or Spanish

- Request updated information about health plans in your area

- Hear recorded answers to frequently asked questions

Determining eligibility

If you're eligible for Social Security retirement payments, you're usually eligible for Medicare coverage. You (or your spouse) accumulate earnings credits on your annual Social Security wages. One earnings credit equals one calendar quarter. You need 40 quarters (ten years) of Social Security credit to enroll in Medicare Part A without cost and in Part B for $45.50 per month (1999 amount). (Look for more information on Medicare later in this chapter.)

Federal government workers, nonprofit-organization employees, and certain other workers may qualify with fewer than 40 quarters. You may also qualify if you have a disability or a chronic kidney disease.

Tip

Check with your local Social Security office for more information or to enroll in Medicare, or call the Social Security Administration at 800-772-1213. (The TTY-TDD number for the hearing- and speech-impaired is 800-325-0778.)

Automatic enrollment

If you're under 65 and receive Social Security or Railroad Retirement benefits, you're automatically enrolled in Medicare Part A and Part B. About three months before your 65th birthday, HCFA mails your Medicare card to you. If you decide to reject Part B after you receive your Medicare card, follow the instructions that accompany the card.

If you're disabled, you are automatically enrolled in Part A and Part B of Medicare beginning in your 25th month of disability. HCFA mails your card to you about three months before you are entitled to Medicare.

Part A and Part B each cover a different set of expenses. The next two sections explain the benefits and costs for each part. All dollar amounts shown are for 1999; figures may change from year to year.

Original Medicare Plan Part A: Covering hospitalization

Medicare's Part A (hospital insurance) covers hospital services, care in skilled nursing facilities, and home health and hospice care services after you're discharged from the hospital. Members of Medicare Part A pay the following premiums:

- Eligible individuals (with 40 quarters of Social Security coverage) pay no premium.

- Individuals with 30 to 39 quarters of Social Security coverage pay $170 per month ($187.00 if you're a late enrollee).

- Ineligible individuals (with fewer than 30 quarters of Social Security coverage) pay $309 per month ($339.90 if you're a late enrollee).

You are a late enrollee if you enroll in Part B after your eligibility period expires. The seven-month eligibility period includes the three months before your 65th birthday, the month of your 65th birthday, and the three months after the month of your 65th birthday. The next opportunity for you to enroll in Part B is during the general enrollment period, from January 1 to March 31 of each year, with coverage beginning July 1. If you wait more than 12 months after the initial enrollment period, you pay an additional 10 percent of the premium. This surcharge applies for a period that is twice as long as enrollment was delayed.

Medicare determines benefits based on a *benefit period*. A benefit period starts the day you're admitted to a hospital or skilled nursing facility. It ends after 60 consecutive days (including the day you're discharged) without hospital inpatient or skilled nursing facility care. If you stay in a skilled nursing facility, a benefit period ends after 60 consecutive days without skilled nursing care.

In each benefit period, Medicare limits the number of days it will help pay for inpatient hospital and skilled nursing facility care. After you exceed the benefit period limit, you must pay for all charges for each additional day of care. After you end a benefit period, a new one begins, with renewed hospital and skilled nursing facility benefits. The number of benefit periods you can have is unlimited.

You are entitled to 60 nonrenewable *reserve days*. You may use reserve days to help pay the bill if you are in the hospital for more than 90 days in a benefit period.

Part A's benefits for inpatient hospital insurance include:

■ **Days 1-60:** You pay a deductible of $768 per benefit period; Medicare pays the rest. **Note:** For days 21-100, Part A also pays coinsurance of $96 a day in a skilled nursing facility.

- **Days 61-90:** You pay coinsurance of $192 a day; Medicare pays the rest.

- **Days 91-150:** You pay $384 a day for each nonrenewable, lifetime reserve day; Medicare pays the rest. (You have a maximum of 60 reserve days, and you may use them only once.)

- **Days 151 and beyond:** You pay all costs; Medicare pays nothing.

Check the Medicaid section later in this chapter for information on additional sources of medical cost reimbursement.

When you enter the hospital for covered care, the hospital must give you a document called *An Important Message from Medicare,* which explains your rights as a Medicare hospital patient. If you don't get a copy, be sure to ask for one. Also ask the billing department for assistance in getting the most benefit from your health insurance coverage.

Original Medicare Plan Part B: Covering medical expenses

Medicare's Part B (medical insurance) covers medical services other than hospitalization. It helps pay doctors and outpatient hospital care. Part B also pays for some other medical services that Part A doesn't cover, including the following:

- Physical and occupational therapy

- Flu, pneumonia, and hepatitis B shots

- X rays and laboratory tests

- Mammograms, and Pap smears to screen for cervical cancer

- Outpatient mental health services

- Artificial limbs and eyes

- Durable medical equipment, including wheelchairs, walkers, hospital beds, and oxygen equipment prescribed for home use by a doctor

- Kidney dialysis and kidney transplants; under limited circumstances, heart, lung, and liver transplants in a Medicare-approved facility

- Medical supplies and items such as ostomy bags, surgical dressings, splints, and casts

Medicare Part B doesn't cover several medical services and items, such as routine physicals, most dental care, dentures, hearing aids, and most prescription drugs. Part B covers eyeglasses only for corrective lenses after cataract surgery.

Members of Medicare Part B pay a monthly premium of $45.50. If you enrolled late (see previous explanation), your premium goes up by 10 percent for each 12-month period you could have been enrolled but weren't.

Part B's members pay an annual deductible of $100. After you pay the $100 deductible, Medicare pays 80 percent of the approved charges for covered services for the rest of the year. (An *approved charge* is the amount that Medicare decides the service is worth. This amount may differ from the actual amount on your bill.) You pay the balance of the hospital's charges. Medicare pays 50 percent for approved outpatient mental health services, and members pay the balance. Members also pay for all charges for services and supplies that Medicare doesn't cover.

Medicare + Choice (Medicare Plus Choice, Medicare Part C)

The Balanced Budget Act of 1997 changed the Medicare program. This law, effective in 1999, includes Medicare + Choice, which expands the Medicare health plan options to include a broader range of plans. You can choose between Original Medicare — a fee-for-service program (see Chapter 1) available to all Medicare beneficiaries — and a managed care organization that has a contract with Medicare. Medicare HMOs are available in many parts of the United States. With Medicare + Choice, Medicare pays the managed care organization to provide medical services to you. In addition, Medicare + Choice offers some preventive care services to help you stay healthy, at no extra cost.

In many ways, the Medicare + Choice managed care plan is like the Original Medicare with an attached Medigap policy (see the next section). Some of these Medicare managed care plans offer services that a Medigap policy doesn't cover. The downside is that generally you can see only doctors and hospitals that belong to the HMO.

To enroll in Medicare + Choice health plan options:

- You must have Medicare Parts A and B.

- You must *not* have end-stage renal disease.

Whether you remain in the Original Medicare plan or choose a Medicare HMO, you're still in the Medicare program and will receive all the Medicare covered services.

Medigap and Medicare SELECT

Original Medicare doesn't pay every medical expense you incur. So, you may want to consider private supplemental insurance policies, such as Medigap policies or Medicare SELECT, to add the extra coverage you need.

Medigap

Although both state and federal governments regulate Medigap insurance policies, Medigap is not government sponsored. Private insurance companies and consumer groups, such as the AARP (American Association of Retired Persons), sell Medigap policies to fill the gaps in the Original Medicare plan coverage. Premiums for Medigap policies are kept to a minimum because the policies cover only the gaps left by Medicare. (Sticking with a Medigap policy makes good sense. Otherwise, you buy another supplemental policy that may cover more than you need and may be more expensive.)

Tip

Call the Medicare hotline at 800-638-6833 (TTY/TDD 800-820-1202 for the hearing or speech impaired) for more information on supplemental insurance policies (Medigap). Call your state insurance office for the names of companies that are licensed to sell Medigap policies in your state. To find your state health insurance contact, check with the National Association of Insurance Commissioners (see the Resource Center for contact information).

The federal government has authorized ten standardized Medigap policies — labeled Plans A through J — which means that the insurance coverage for a specific plan, such as Plan D, is the same from one company to another and from one state to another. Plans A through J represent a wide range in coverage. Plan A offers the most basic supplement to Medicare coverage. Plan B (not to be confused with Medicare Part B) offers the same provisions as in Plan A, along with additional specified provisions, and so on through Plan J. Plan J offers the most coverage of the Medigap plans and is usually the most expensive.

The availability of these plans depends on where you live: Your state may offer all or just a few of the standard policies. If an insurance company wants to sell Medigap policies, it must sell at least Plan A.

An insurance company cannot legally sell you more than one Medigap policy. Because Medigap policies are designed to fill in the gaps left by Medicare coverage, you don't need more than one Medigap policy.

Medigap policies normally pay most or all of the Medicare coinsurance amounts. They may also cover Medicare deductibles. Some plans pay part or all of the following:

- Outpatient prescription drugs (plans H, I, and J)

- Preventive care (plans E and J)

- Emergency medical care in a foreign country (plans C through J)

- Limited coverage for home health care (plans D, G, I, and J)

Medigap policies don't cover long-term care. When your financial resources are depleted, you may meet your state's eligibility requirements for Medicaid. If so, Medicaid helps pay for long-term care.

Signing up for Medigap benefits while you're enrolled in a Medicare HMO is duplicate coverage. Medigap policies are designed to pay benefits associated with fee-for-service plans.

Certain consumer protection regulations, including a 30-day money-back guarantee and a guarantee of renewability, govern the insurance companies that sell Medigap policies. The Health Insurance Portability and Accountability Act (HIPAA) regulations — see Chapter 3 — apply to Medigap to govern pre-existing condition waiting periods.

Medicare SELECT

Insurance companies and managed care plans throughout the country can sell Medicare SELECT, another type of Medicare supplemental health insurance plan. A Medicare SELECT policy must meet all of the same requirements that a Medigap policy must meet, and it must be one of the ten standardized benefit packages (A through J). The only difference is that with Medicare SELECT, you must use hospitals and doctors within a network to be eligible for full benefits. (Emergencies are an exception.) Medicare SELECT policy premiums are usually lower because of this restriction.

Medicaid

Medicaid — Title XIX of the Social Security Act — is a program that provides medical assistance for certain individuals, such as children, the aged, the blind, the disabled, and people who are eligible to receive other federal assistance. It is a joint federal and state health insurance program, developed to assist states in providing adequate medical care to eligible needy persons. The federal government set broad national guidelines for states to use in designing their Medicaid programs. Each state, however, can do the following:

- Establish its own requirements for eligibility

- Decide on the type, amount, length, and range of services

- Set the rate of payment for services

- Administer its own Medicaid program

With the states' flexibility in setting up the details of their own Medicaid plans, plans vary a great deal from state to state, as well as within each state over time. So if you move to another state, don't assume that you automatically meet the new state's Medicaid eligibility requirements. You may have to reapply for Medicaid coverage; acceptance may take two or three months. If you have a gap in coverage between the old and new plans, you are responsible for any expenses that you incur.

If you qualify for both Medicare and Medicaid, Medicaid covers most of your health care costs.

Always send your medical bills to Medicare first. Medicare sends the unpaid part of the bill to your state Medicaid program for additional payment.

States determine eligibility for Medicaid by examining a person's disability or age and financial need. You may have to reduce your assets to the allowable limits, which is called *spending down.* Because Medicaid is based on financial need, Medicare is considered a resource that you must use before Medicaid kicks in.

When you apply for Medicaid, be ready to reveal all your assets and sources of income. Not telling the state about all your assets is fraud, which is subject to criminal penalties.

If your income is limited — as defined by your state — Medicaid may help pay for Medicare premiums, deductibles, and coinsurance.

Medicaid offers some assistance in various categories of *dual eligibles.* Dual eligibles are individuals who are entitled to Medicare Part A and/or Part B and are eligible for some form of Medicaid benefit.

Medicaid has eight categories of dual eligibles, defined by criteria such as Medicare eligibility, income level, and the dollar amount of resources in relation to Supplemental Security Income (SSI). (SSI is a social assistance program that pays monthly cash benefits to individuals who are at least 65, or who are blind or disabled, and who have limited income and resources.)

If you receive Supplemental Security Income (SSI) payments from Social Security, you are eligible for Medicaid. Contact your state Medicaid office for application information. In addition, contact your state or local welfare, social service, or Medicaid agency for more information about whether you qualify for financial help. You may find the appropriate telephone numbers in a "government" section of your local telephone directory under "Health and Human Services"; if not, call directory assistance. State Medicaid toll-free numbers are listed on the Web at www.hcfa.gov/MEDICAID/ obs5.htm.

Children's Health Insurance Program (CHIP)

Parents whose income is too large to be eligible for Medicaid and yet too small to afford private health insurance can turn to their state's Children's Health Insurance Program (CHIP) to cover their uninsured children. (CHIP, or SCHIP — State Children's Health Insurance Program — is also known as Title XXI, part of the federal Balanced Budget Act of 1997.) Every state and five U.S. territories have CHIP programs. Each runs its own federally funded CHIP program, so the programs vary.

States must ensure that CHIP funds only cover children who are currently uninsured.

Find out how CHIP affects you. Call the toll-free number, 877-543-7669, to find your state's toll-free CHIP phone number, or look for your state's number at www.hcfa.gov/ init/chipinfo.htm.

CHAPTER 7

DEALING WITH CLAIMS

IN THIS CHAPTER

- Keeping track of family health history and medical records

- Understanding coordination of benefits

- Increasing your chances of getting your claim processed the first time around

This chapter stresses the importance of keeping good medical records to make sure that you file accurate claims. This chapter also explains the standards that determine how insurance plans determine which plan pays first. If you have more than one insurer, knowing the order in which to file your claim can save time and money.

Keeping Good Records

With accurate, up-to-date records, filling out the *claim form* (a request to pay your medical expenses) should be simple and painless. Correct information on the claim form also lessens the chance that the insurance company rejects your claim or returns it for additional information.

For each person in your family, keep a record — in chronological order — of each event related to a particular condition. The record should include enough information to make reconstructing the details of a condition easy for you. Include summaries and dates of pertinent telephone conversations and correspondence. Keep the form in a file folder and add the appropriate paperwork — copies of bills, receipts, correspondence, prescriptions, and the like — to the file.

Table 7-1 shows an example of such a record. You can change or add to the categories to reflect your own needs. Fill out the record in diary fashion, entering first the date of the next event with the appropriate corresponding information and notes. Add pages as necessary.

Table 7-1: Troy Family Health Record

Claim Information	Family Member
Name of patient	Helena
Date of birth	10/9/54
Social Security number	111-22-3333
Name of insurance company	Happy Health Insurance
Insurance policy group number	0700-131886
Your insurance ID number	123-45-6789
Date of service	1/1/2000
Diagnosis	Flu
Name of provider, correspondent	Dr. Gary
Address and telephone number for provider, correspondent	Dean Medical Center, 1541 Market; 555-4321
Description of services, prescriptions, telephone conversations, correspondence	Saw Helena, prescribed light diet, bed rest
Notes, comments, questions	Requested medication but the doctor thought we should wait a day or two
Cost of service	$65
Amount you paid	$15 copay
Amount submitted to the insurance company	$50
How much the insurance company paid	Nothing: Applied the $50 to the deductible
Balance due	$50
Date paid balance due	2/5/2000

Continued

Table 7-1: Troy Family Health Record *(continued)*

Claim Information	Family Member
Date	1/5/2000
Description of services, prescriptions, telephone conversations, correspondence	Saw Dr. Gary again, who said that Helena didn't need any medication; she looked much better
Cost of service	$30 for follow-up visit
And so on	

You may also want to keep another set of records for each person in your family that covers health history, showing illnesses, injuries, medications, immunizations, and their corresponding dates. For a complete family history, record your parents' and other relatives' health information as well.

Ask your provider for a copy of your file — including results of lab work and tests — which you can pick up in person or have sent to you at home. Occasionally, the lab or test results that you get by phone may differ from the written results. Add the information from the file to your family medical file.

In addition to helping you file a complete and accurate claim, keeping good records serves other purposes. If you're applying for a new health insurance plan, for instance, you may need records as proof of creditable coverage. (Refer to Chapter 3 for more information about creditable coverage.) Save the following:

■ Pay stubs showing deductions for health insurance premiums

■ Copies of premium payments

■ Other evidence of health care coverage

Managing Coordination of Benefits (COB)

Some people have health insurance coverage under more than one group plan. You may have coverage under a spouse's plan, for example, as well as under your own plan. Group plans use *coordination of benefits (COB)* to eliminate any chance of duplicating benefits when you submit a claim to both insurance companies. In such cases, the combined benefits that the two plans pay add up to no more than the amount submitted for covered charges.

The insurance industry has established standards for determining the order in which two or more insurers must pay for covered services. The insurer that must pay first is the *primary* or *principal insurer;* the second plan is the *secondary* or *lesser insurer.* The following rules determine which plan is primary and which plan is secondary:

■ If one plan has COB and the other plan doesn't have COB, the plan without COB is primary (pays first).

■ If one plan is for an active employee and the other plan is for a retired person, the plan for the active employee is primary.

■ If the patient is the policyholder in one plan and is insured as a dependent under the other plan, the patient's own plan is primary (unless the patient is a retired person and the holder of the other plan is an active employee).

■ If the patient has more than one plan in his or her name, the plan in which the patient has been enrolled the longest is primary.

■ If a child is covered by both (not divorced) parents' group plans, the plan of the parent with the birthday that falls on the earliest date of the year is primary (the *birthday rule*). If both parents' birthdays fall on the same day, the plan that began first is primary. The birthday rule doesn't take into account the actual year the parents were born, just the month.

■ Unless a court order states otherwise, if a child of divorced parents is covered by both parents' group plans, the plan of the custodial parent is primary. (When parents remarry, the plan of the custodial parent is primary; the plan of the custodial stepparent is secondary; and the plan of the noncustodial parent is third in line.)

The standards also regulate the amounts that each insurer must pay. The primary insurer pays as it normally would for covered charges. The primary insurer then submits a statement of the benefits it paid to the secondary insurer before the secondary insurer pays. The secondary insurer picks up the charges for the deductible and coinsurance or copayment. The secondary carrier also pays for benefits covered in the secondary plan but not covered by the primary plan.

If you have more than one health insurance policy, be sure that you understand how the plans will coordinate your benefits. Carefully check each plan to understand how and when to submit insurance claims, as well as which plan to send them to first.

The definition of "coordination of benefits" refers to group plans only. Individual plans don't usually include a COB clause, although every state has its own regulations governing COB with individual plans. In this case, a person with both a group plan and an individual plan who submits the same medical expenses to both plans may receive duplicate benefits. Although this prospect may sound like a good idea, remember that premiums for individual plans are very high, so you may not come out ahead financially.

Submitting a Claim

To ask the insurance company to pay your providers — or to reimburse you if you have already paid your providers — you submit a claim form. Each health insurance company usually has its own claim forms that it provides to members.

Sometimes insurers accept forms directly from a health care provider's office as long as the forms include all the information necessary for processing the claim.

If you belong to an HMO or a PPO, you probably don't need to fill out a claim form for office visits or hospitalization. You simply show your member card. If you're a member of a PPO and use a provider outside the network or if you have a fee-for-service plan, you probably do have to complete a claim form, although sometimes your health care provider fills out the claim form for you.

When you fill out a claim form, a couple of paragraphs in fine print require your signature. One of these paragraphs is the *assignment of benefits*. When you sign the assignment of benefits, you authorize the insurance company to pay claim benefits directly to the health care provider. If you already paid your provider and want the insurance company to reimburse you, don't sign the assignment of benefits.

Claim forms indicate what information you need to fill in and which information your provider needs to enter. The patient or policyholder usually fills in the following information:

- Name of policyholder, address, and Social Security number

- Name of the insurance company, group number, and the policyholder's ID number

- Patient's name, address, date of birth, sex, and relationship to the policyholder

- Patient's marital status and work status (employed or student)

- Employer's name and phone number

- Whether the claim is due to an injury; if so, date of injury and whether the injury occurred at work

- Name, address, and phone number of other insurance company covering patient

- Whether the patient has Medicare coverage (see Chapter 6)

- Signature to authorize release of information and assignment of benefits

When you sign the authorization to release information, you're giving the insurance company the right to get any and all information relevant to your claim from your health care providers.

Either the patient (or policyholder) or the health care provider may have to fill in the following:

- Date of first sign of illness, or date of accident

- Date of previous instance of same or similar illness

- Dates the patient is unable to work in current occupation

- Name and ID number of referring physician

- Hospitalization dates

The health care provider usually fills in the following:

- Diagnosis or nature of illness or injury

- Dates of service, procedures, and charges

- Federal tax ID number

- Patient account number

- Whether the provider accepts assignment of benefits

- Amount paid and balance due

- Provider signature and date

Double-check that all information you enter on the claim form is legible and correct. Sign and date the form. Make a photocopy for your records and attach copies of itemized bills and/or receipts. (Photocopies are important, especially if the claim is lost and you have to resubmit it.) Bills and receipts must include the patient's name, date, service, and charge. If the receipt is for a prescription, it must also include the pre-scription number, the doctor who ordered the prescription, and the pharmacy's name and address. Mail the claim form and note the date you send it to your insurance company.

Tip

Send *all* your bills to the insurance company, even if you don't think they're covered. If you have an expense that you can apply to your deductible, the only way to get credit for that expense is to send the bill to the insurer.

Warning

Check your insurance plan carefully for the claim submission deadline — usually 90 days from the date the charges are incurred. If you submit your claim after the deadline, the insurer won't consider your claim.

After the insurance company receives your claim, it sends you an *Explanation of Benefits (EOB)* or *Explanation of Medicare Benefits (EOMB)* to let you know how much it will pay. For each procedure you submit through your claim form, the EOB shows the fee that the insurance company allows. If the company doesn't pay a benefit on a procedure, the EOB gives the reason for denying benefits. You may appeal a claim if you disagree with the amount paid. See Chapter 8 for infor-mation on appealing a claim.

TROUBLESHOOTING INSURANCE PROBLEMS

IN THIS CHAPTER

■ Appealing claims that are rejected

■ Distinguishing between accidents and illnesses in the emergency room

Sometimes you may disagree with your health insurance plan's payment of benefits. This chapter teaches you how to appeal and where to turn when that happens.

Some health insurance plans attempt to control costs by refusing payment for emergency room care unless you first get permission from your doctor. Sometimes emergency room staff delays treatment while they check your insurance coverage. Legislation now establishes certain rights for emergency room patients, which minimizes these kinds of restrictions. This chapter explains your rights to emergency room treatment under these laws.

Appealing a Claim

If you object to the way your insurer paid your claim, start by calling your plan's benefits administrator, if you have one, or check with your human resources department. If your objections are still unresolved, your next step is to *file an appeal* — a means of objecting to the way the insurer paid your claim and requesting the insurer to reconsider the claim.

Check your health insurance policy for a section on the appeals process. Your plan may spell out each step that you must follow to appeal your claim. Be aware of deadlines that you must meet to resubmit a claim, or you may lose your right to appeal.

Follow up on the response you receive from the insurer. Read it carefully and make sure that the insurer bases its decision on the correct information. If you discover that some of the information you submitted on your original claim is incorrect or inaccurate, notify the insurer in writing of the correction.

Mail correspondence by certified mail with a return receipt to confirm that the insurer received your letter.

If the insurer continues to deny benefits, submit copies of the claim, correspondence, notes, and the relevant pages of your policy to your state's insurance department. Remember to include your policy or claim number. Write a cover letter explaining in detail why you think the insurer did not properly pay benefits for your medical expenses.

The department of insurance notifies the insurance company of your complaint. The insurer must then respond to the state insurance department within a specified period, usually 10 to 30 days. After the insurance department receives the insurer's response, it investigates and comes up with a solution, if possible. Expect this process to take at least 30 days (longer if the case is complicated).

As you work through the appeals process, keep in mind that each state has its own laws — usually referred to as the Unfair Claims Settlement Practices Act — to protect you from unfair and deceptive practices in the insurance industry.

For more information on your particular state's laws, contact your state's insurance department. To find your state health insurance contact, check with the National Association of

Insurance Commissioners (see the Resource Center for contact information).

Although the insurance protection laws differ from state to state, most of them have the following provisions in common. The laws state that insurance companies

- Must not intentionally misrepresent facts or provisions relating to coverage under your policy, such as stating that a condition is covered when it isn't.

- Must acknowledge your claim and act promptly in response to your communications about your claim.

- Must put into action standards for timely investigation and processing of claims.

- Must not attempt to influence payment of a claim you make under one benefit provision (such as a hospital benefit) by delaying payment under another (such as a prescription drug benefit) when the amount the company owes you is clear.

- Must not delay an investigation or payment of claims by asking you for reports or forms that are unnecessary or contain information that you've already submitted.

- Must not force you to file a lawsuit to recover money due under an insurance policy by offering you considerably less than the money ultimately recovered in a lawsuit.

- Must not, as a policy, appeal arbitration awards in your favor to force you to accept a settlement amount or compromise for less than the amount awarded in arbitration. Both sides choose one independent third party, such as a judge or lawyer, to determine the outcome (arbitrate). The decision the arbitrator makes is usually final.

- Must not refuse to pay your claim or delay payment without conducting a reasonable investigation and giving you a valid reason.

If you think that your insurance company is violating the Unfair Claims Practices Act, talk to a claims supervisor at the company and explain your concern. If that doesn't help resolve your problem, file a complaint with your state's insurance department.

The state insurance department can help only if the insurance company has broken the law. It can't force the insurer to provide a benefit that isn't in the health insurance policy. Many state insurance departments try to resolve the complaint by phone before the consumer resorts to filing a formal complaint.

If you hire a lawyer to resolve your complaint, the state insurance department won't speak with you directly. As your legal representative, your lawyer speaks for you.

If their finding is against the insurance company, state insurance departments have the authority to impose penalties on an insurance company, ranging from assessing a fine to revoking the company's state license.

Recognizing Your Emergency Room Rights

The Emergency Medical Treatment and Active Labor Act of 1998 (EMTALA) states that hospitals must give appropriate care to people regardless of their ability to pay, including people whose health insurance coverage restricts emergency room benefits. Hospital staff can't postpone examining a patient while checking on insurance coverage or while trying to get permission from a doctor in the patient's health plan network to examine or treat the patient.

Individual state laws may offer rights in addition to the rights in EMTALA. Some states have a regulation that requires insurance companies to pay for emergency room care if a *prudent*

layperson (a person with an average knowledge of health and medicine) acting reasonably would consider the situation a medical emergency.

Emergency room staff must do a medical exam before sending you to a clinic or doctor's office. The exam determines whether you need immediate care and avoids putting your health at risk. If emergency room doctors determine that you have an emergency medical condition, they must stabilize or appropriately transfer you to another medical facility.

EMTALA defines an *emergency medical condition* as a medical condition with symptoms so severe that you could reasonably expect the lack of immediate medical attention to result in

- Seriously jeopardizing a patient's or unborn child's health (in the case of a pregnant woman)
- Seriously harming any bodily functions or parts

When a pregnant woman is having contractions, EMTALA considers it an emergency when

- There isn't enough time to safely transfer the pregnant woman to another hospital before giving birth
- Transferring the pregnant woman may threaten her health or safety or the health or safety of the unborn child

If your condition doesn't meet the definition of "emergency medical condition," the hospital emergency room doesn't have to treat you.

CHAPTER 9

KNOWING YOUR CONSUMER RIGHTS

IN THIS CHAPTER

- ■ Protecting the privacy of your medical records
- ■ Recognizing and avoiding insurance fraud

In these days of lightning-quick transfer of information and boundless computer storage capacity, doctors, employers, insurance companies, and others can gain access to your medical records quite easily. Concern arises when these entities use your personal information to deny you health insurance coverage or even employment. This chapter discusses ways to keep abuses like these in check.

Insurance fraud costs everyone more and more, both in dollars and in inadequate medical treatment. Keep reading to find out how to recognize, avoid, and report insurance fraud.

Consumer Protection and Confidentiality

Medical records may contain information about your family history, substance abuse, sexual behavior, and mental illness. You depend on these records being kept confidential. But think about the number of people who might have access to your medical records, just in the course of one visit to a health care provider: doctor, nurse, receptionist, billing office, pharmacist, health insurer. If you're hospitalized or you visit the emergency room, the number of people increases. If your employer administers your benefits, human resource staff members may also have access to your medical records. What's more, the Department of Health and Human

Services plans to set up a "unique health identifier" number to link all your health records to one, universal number ID.

All of this probably doesn't sound as though your records are "confidential." They're not.

Medical Information Bureau (MIB)

The Medical Information Bureau (MIB), a clearinghouse for information on individual medical records, provides medical information about individuals to approximately 600 life insurance companies, many of which also offer health and disability coverage. When an individual applies for life, health, or disability insurance, the applicant's medical records are likely to become part of MIB's database. Sometimes members of small groups, late enrollees, and applicants requesting additional coverage may end up in the database as well.

Insurers pay a membership fee to MIB and a fee each time they verify applicants' information. Insurers also report individuals' medical conditions to MIB to add to its database. When you apply for an insurance policy and the insurer checks with MIB, you may end up paying higher premiums because of information MIB reports to the insurer. In an extreme case, you may not be hired for a job or you may lose a job because of a condition that shows up on your medical record.

Insurance companies are supposed to notify you if they intend to check your record at MIB when you apply for insurance. Ask your agent when you apply whether the company uses MIB.

Protecting your privacy

You can take steps to protect the confidentiality of your medical records:

- Ask your health care providers, in writing, for a copy of your medical records. Correct any errors. Find out to whom these providers give access to your records.

- Instead of signing a blanket release waiver, give permission to release only records that relate to a specific treatment or condition.

- Be stingy with the information — including your Social Security number — that you give out on surveys and questionnaires, especially over the phone.

- Check whether MIB has a record on you and make sure that the record is accurate, which is your right under the Fair Credit Reporting Act. You can write to MIB at P.O. Box 105, Essex Station, Boston, MA 02112; phone 617-426-3660; Web site www.mib.com.

- Tell MIB in writing not to release your information without your notarized consent. Withdraw all prior consent.

- Get copies of company policies covering medical records if your employer is self-insured and therefore subject to ERISA regulations. Storing medical records in personnel files is illegal — make sure that the company policies specify that.

- Giving your doctor all the information necessary for your treatment is important. However, consider holding back information that isn't relevant to your health.

- Call or write your congressional representative. Ask for a medical privacy law that limits medical information to health care providers and insurers and doesn't include a universal "health identification number."

Federal law states that medical records are confidential. Under the Americans with Disabilities Act, companies must not use medical records to make employment decisions.

Employers can find out even more from credit records that reflect billing for health care services and from bankruptcy records.

Genetic testing, which can indicate predisposition to inherited diseases, may become another area of concern in the privacy issue. If your insurers pay for genetic testing, their records will include the results.

Insurance Fraud

Insurance fraud by policyholders and others is on the upswing, and people aren't very outraged about it. Some people think they're just getting even with a large company, rather than committing a crime, when they defraud an insurance company. But everyone ends up paying for losses due to fraud through increased insurance premiums, higher taxes for government-sponsored programs such as Medicare, more expensive doctor visits, and more expensive prescription drugs.

Both patients and providers can commit fraud. Insurance frauds include

- Adding to claims expenses for services not delivered or inflating the cost of services.

- Lying on applications or withholding material information.

- Submitting false claims.

- Faking injuries and illnesses.

- Medical quackery (pretending to practice medicine).

- Obtaining the same prescription drugs from several doctors.

- False coverage schemes, such as when an "insurance company" accepts your premiums but doesn't pay your claims.

- Substituting a covered diagnosis for a routine checkup.

Insurance companies are fighting back to a greater and greater extent. Insurers are diligently pursuing perpetrators of fraud in every way possible, including using special investigative units and high-tech data tracking. The Department of Health and Human Services (HHS) asks that Medicare recipients review their Medicare statements. If Medicare recipients find a suspicious charge, they should call their doctor or the HHS fraud watchdog line at 800-447-8477.

Don't be a victim of fraud. Keep your eyes open and watch for the following:

- Free testing or screening offers that involve showing your health insurance ID card or Medicare card

- Doctors or other providers who want you to sign a claim form before providing a service

- Doctors or other providers who explain that they can prepare a bill so a charge that an insurance company doesn't usually cover will be covered

- Medical laboratories or health clinics that bill for tests or other services that they didn't provide

- Doctors who bill for inpatient hospital services on dates you weren't in the hospital

Keep fraud at a minimum with these measures:

- Ask your doctor and other providers whether the treatments and services they prescribe are medically necessary and what options are available.

- Always check carefully the Explanation of Benefits (EOB) that you receive from your insurance company or from Medicare. Look for charges for services that you didn't receive, treatments that were more complex than the ones you received, and multiple charges for a service that you received only once.

- When you buy health insurance coverage from an agent or company you're not familiar with, contact your state's department of insurance to verify that the company is licensed to operate in your state. Don't buy insurance from an agent who offers you a kickback. Report these types of fraud to your state insurance department.

- Read the fine print in mail promotions. Report deceptive mail promotions to your local postmaster.

- Don't trust a company that wants you to pay your premiums in cash or pay a full year's worth of premiums at one time.

- Don't give in to "last chance" opportunities to buy a policy.

- Never sign a blank insurance form.

- Have someone you trust — perhaps a knowledgeable friend, accountant, or attorney — review any policy you're unsure of.

Seniors may be especially vulnerable to fraud. When seniors buy Medigap policies, they sometimes fall prey to crooked salespeople who try to sell policies with too little or improper coverage or to people who don't need coverage.

CHAPTER 10
CHOOSING A NEW HEALTH INSURANCE PLAN

IN THIS CHAPTER

- Deciding what's important to you in selecting an insurance plan

- Using a health insurance checklist to sift through the options

The vast number of choices and decisions involved in selecting a health insurance plan makes the task complicated and confusing. This chapter replaces confusion with understanding and clarity by examining some of the major factors that you will eventually rely on to make your choice. The Checklist in Table 10-1 at the end of this chapter gives you a way to track your priorities and needs as you learn about health insurance plans.

Refer to the Checklist often and change your rankings as needed. Check the Resource Center at the end of this book for organizations and literature to aid in your research.

Drawing Up Your Selection Criteria

The first step in selecting a health insurance plan is determining your priorities and needs. The next step is comparing those priorities and needs with the coverage that a given health insurance plan offers. To make the selection process manageable, the next sections explain some of the major features that make up a health insurance plan.

Covering yourself, your spouse, and your dependents

If you're employed and married or have a domestic partner, you may have some flexibility in choosing secondary coverage under a spouse's or partner's plan. For example, two adults who each have individual coverage may pay less in premiums than if both are covered under one policy with a family plan.

If you and your spouse are each covered by a group plan, you may be able to get secondary (additional) coverage under the other's plan, or you may decide to forego secondary coverage and stick with one plan per person. Or one spouse may drop his or her employer's insurance altogether and obtain coverage under the other's policy. (Be sure that neither plan has provisions that prohibit this choice.) Weigh the cost of each option against the coverage you get before making a decision.

Some families include unmarried domestic partners. Check out your plan's policies regarding coverage for domestic partners, but don't be surprised if coverage isn't available.

The issue of health insurance for domestic partners has no national legislation, nor does any state have regulations covering its employees' domestic partners.

To cover a person under your health insurance plan, that person must be considered a *dependent*. The definition of dependent is based on your plan's legal requirements concerning financial support. (In an employer-sponsored plan, the employer may also have input into the definition of dependent.) Some plans consider a child a dependent only if the child meets all of the following very specific criteria:

- The child is your responsibility by birth or legal adoption, or the child is a stepchild or a foster child.

- The policyholder provides more than 50 percent of financial support and maintenance for this child.

■ The policyholder can claim the child as an exemption on his or her federal income tax return.

A child is considered a dependent if a legal court order mandates that the policyholder must provide coverage for the child. Other individuals may be considered dependents if they satisfy IRS requirements.

Health insurance plans' regulations regarding coverage for children and/or other dependents may vary greatly, so check out the plans carefully. To make administration simple and consistent, some companies use some variation of the *birthday rule,* in which the primary coverage for eligible children is through the plan of the parent whose birthday falls in the earlier month of the year. For example, a parent born in May 1954 would assume coverage for the children, even though the spouse born in September 1950 is older.

Selecting doctors and hospitals

Many health insurance plans have an arrangement between the insurer and a selected group (or *network*) of doctors and hospitals and other health care providers. Such plans offer significant financial incentives to policyholders to use the providers in that network, including reducing your benefits when you use doctors and hospitals outside the network.

Before you decide to buy a particular health insurance plan, find out which doctors and hospitals are included in the plan's network. Use this section to evaluate those doctors and hospitals. If they don't satisfy your needs, evaluate other doctors and hospitals with this section and then look for a plan that uses the doctors and hospitals of your choice.

Consider the following factors when you assess doctors and hospitals in relation to a health insurance plan.

■ **Location of doctors and hospitals:** If you prefer to deal with a nearby doctor or hospital, check to see whether these providers are part of the network of the plan you're considering. If you travel much, find out what the plan's benefits are if you need to consult doctors or visit hospitals outside the plan's provider network.

Doctors are usually associated with a particular hospital. When selecting a doctor, keep in mind that you usually end up using the services of the hospital with which that doctor is affiliated.

■ **Primary care physician (PCP):** A *primary care physician* is a doctor who provides or authorizes all care for a patient. Most HMOs and PPOs (see Chapter 1 for more information) require their members to choose a primary care physician.

If freedom of choice in selecting your primary care physician isn't that important to you, an HMO or PPO may be a good choice for you.

If you're already happy with a doctor who isn't part of a plan network, a fee-for-service plan (also known as an *indemnity plan*) may be a good choice for you. This type of plan allows you the greatest choice of doctors and hospitals. You can also ask your out-of-network provider to consider joining a network — check with your benefits administrator for the forms.

Some doctors require payment at the time of service. Others offer a grace period for payment. Still other doctors file your insurance claim for you or file directly with the insurer. If you prefer not to pay the doctor and wait for your insurance company to reimburse you, find out what the doctor's policies are and whether you can make special arrangements for payment.

■ **Specialists:** Some plans require that you get a referral from your primary care physician prior to each time you see a specialist. Getting a referral usually involves a visit to the primary care physician for diagnosis and perhaps treatment to see whether the more expensive visit to the specialist is necessary. Check to see whether your preferred specialist is in the plan's network or whether the network has a specialist who deals with your particular condition. Using an out-of-network specialist may cost you more.

■ **Hospitals' quality of care:** Most hospitals participate in an accreditation program that the Joint Commission on Accreditation of Healthcare Organizations (JCAHO) administers. This organization surveys hospitals every three years to assure that they meet specific quality standards for staff and equipment, as well as for their success in treating and curing patients. Make sure that the hospitals within your plan's network are accredited.

Call your state department of health, health care council, or hospital association to find out what kind of consumer information is available. You may also call or visit the hospital's quality assurance staff. They should be able to tell you how they oversee and work to improve the hospital's quality of care. In addition, ask them about recent patient satisfaction surveys.

■ **Nursing staff:** Ask the hospital's nursing staff how the staff is structured. In *functional nursing,* each nurse is responsible for particular tasks. In *primary nursing,* each nurse is responsible for a certain number of patients, generally resulting in better care. The patient-to-nurse ratio should not exceed six to one. Check that the hospital in your plan's network has a structure and a patient-to-nurse ratio that provides optimal care.

■ **General or specialty hospital:** If you or your dependents have a condition that requires medical staff with specific experience, you may prefer to be affiliated with a specialty hospital, such as a children's hospital. In that case, check whether the specialty hospital you may need is within a plan's network.

- ■ **Other services:** Research some of the services that may be important to you — does the hospital offer community education programs, pre-admission testing services to reduce inpatient time, or a referral network with information about a more specialized facility? Are hospital-affiliated acute care centers (extensions of emergency rooms) located near your home? Is the food edible? Does the hospital accommodate special diets? Learn about the visiting hours and whether lodging is available for parents to stay overnight with their children. Tour the hospital to find out whether the rooms and halls are clean and comfortable and the staff is friendly and helpful.

Waiting for coverage to start

Be sure that you know exactly when your coverage begins. Insurance companies may sometimes impose a waiting period between the time you apply for or enroll in a plan and the date your coverage takes effect. The waiting period — sometimes due to a pre-existing condition — may apply to some or all of a plan's benefits.

If you enroll in a group plan when you begin a new job or when your employer offers an open enrollment period, you usually don't have a waiting period. Individual plans are usually stricter and most likely will impose a waiting period. Generally, you don't begin paying premiums until your waiting period is over.

Keep in mind the kinds of medical care you may need when you're switching insurance companies or plans and be sure that you remain covered, perhaps by extending your current plan and overlapping it with a new one.

Understanding accreditation of health insurance plans

You can check on the quality of the health insurance plan you're considering through your state's department of health or insurance commission or through consumer publications.

Investigate the insurance company itself by checking your library for insurance company ratings by organizations such as The A.M. Best Company, Standard & Poor's, and Moody's. These organizations base their evaluations on the insurance companies' financial records, which may give you an idea of a company's stability. A highly-rated insurance company generally won't go out of business overnight and disappear without paying your claims.

Also check for *accreditation,* which indicates that a plan meets certain national standards set by independent organizations such as the Joint Commission on Accreditation of Health-care Organizations (JCAHO). An insurance company's deci-sion not to participate in an accreditation program does not reflect one way or another on its quality. To find out whether the plan you're interested in is accredited, ask your employer's benefits manager or call the insurance company itself.

One company that offers accreditation of health insurance plans is the National Committee for Quality Assurance (NCQA). This company evaluates a health plan's organiza-tion, structure, and quality improvement process. NCQA also uses the Health Plan Employer Data and Information Set (HEDIS), a group of about 50 factors, to measure plans' quality of care.

Using Your Health Insurance Checklist

Use the Checklist in Table 10-1 to track what's important to you in a health insurance plan. As you work through the

Checklist, keep in mind current medical conditions, as well as the possibility of accidents, serious illnesses, and other surprises that life may throw your way. For now, leave blank the areas that you're unsure about. By the end of the list, you should have a clear and fairly comprehensive picture of what your needs are and what type of health insurance plan will satisfy those needs.

Check one of the boxes to indicate how important each service is to you. The Checklist indicates importance on a scale of 0 to 5 — 0 is for the services that you don't need at all; 5 indicates those that you think you'll need the most.

Use a pencil to fill out the Checklist; as you learn more, your priorities may change. Use the blank lines at the end of the Checklist to add items of special concern to you.

Table 10-1: Checklist for Determining Your Health Insurance Needs

	0	1	2	3	4	5
Choice of doctors	❏	❏	❏	❏	❏	❏
Nearby doctors and hospitals	❏	❏	❏	❏	❏	❏
Out-of-town doctors and hospitals	❏	❏	❏	❏	❏	❏
Costs	❏	❏	❏	❏	❏	❏
Ease of getting an appointment	❏	❏	❏	❏	❏	❏
Minimal paperwork	❏	❏	❏	❏	❏	❏
Waiting period before coverage	❏	❏	❏	❏	❏	❏
Covered medical services	❏	❏	❏	❏	❏	❏
Adult day care	❏	❏	❏	❏	❏	❏
Alternative treatments such as acupuncture, spiritual care, and so on	❏	❏	❏	❏	❏	❏
Ambulance	❏	❏	❏	❏	❏	❏

	0	1	2	3	4	5
Cancer screening (colorectal cancer tests, mammograms, Pap smears, and so on)	❑	❑	❑	❑	❑	❑
Chiropractic	❑	❑	❑	❑	❑	❑
Cholesterol screening	❑	❑	❑	❑	❑	❑
Dental care, braces, and teeth cleaning	❑	❑	❑	❑	❑	❑
Diabetes supplies	❑	❑	❑	❑	❑	❑
Drug and alcohol abuse treatment	❑	❑	❑	❑	❑	❑
Family planning	❑	❑	❑	❑	❑	❑
Hearing examinations, hearing aids	❑	❑	❑	❑	❑	❑
Home health care	❑	❑	❑	❑	❑	❑
Hospice care	❑	❑	❑	❑	❑	❑
Hospital care	❑	❑	❑	❑	❑	❑
Immunizations	❑	❑	❑	❑	❑	❑
Infertility treatment	❑	❑	❑	❑	❑	❑
Inpatient hospital	❑	❑	❑	❑	❑	❑
Maternity care	❑	❑	❑	❑	❑	❑
Medical equipment for home use	❑	❑	❑	❑	❑	❑
Medical tests and X rays	❑	❑	❑	❑	❑	❑
Mental health care	❑	❑	❑	❑	❑	❑
Nursing home care	❑	❑	❑	❑	❑	❑
Office visits to your doctor	❑	❑	❑	❑	❑	❑
Other covered services	❑	❑	❑	❑	❑	❑
Outpatient surgery	❑	❑	❑	❑	❑	❑
Pediatric care	❑	❑	❑	❑	❑	❑
Physical therapy	❑	❑	❑	❑	❑	❑

continued

Table 10-1: Checklist for Determining Your Health Insurance Needs *(continued)*

	0	1	2	3	4	5
Physician visits (in the hospital)	❏	❏	❏	❏	❏	❏
Pre-existing condition care	❏	❏	❏	❏	❏	❏
Prenatal care	❏	❏	❏	❏	❏	❏
Prescription drugs	❏	❏	❏	❏	❏	❏
Preventive care and checkups	❏	❏	❏	❏	❏	❏
Rehabilitation facility care	❏	❏	❏	❏	❏	❏
Skilled nursing care	❏	❏	❏	❏	❏	❏
Smoking cessation counseling	❏	❏	❏	❏	❏	❏
Speech therapy	❏	❏	❏	❏	❏	❏
Surgery (inpatient and outpatient)	❏	❏	❏	❏	❏	❏
Vision care (eyeglasses, contact lenses, examinations, and so on)	❏	❏	❏	❏	❏	❏
Well-baby care	❏	❏	❏	❏	❏	❏
Other needs						
	❏	❏	❏	❏	❏	❏
	❏	❏	❏	❏	❏	❏
	❏	❏	❏	❏	❏	❏
	❏	❏	❏	❏	❏	❏

CLIFFSNOTES REVIEW

Use this CliffsNotes Review to practice what you've learned in this book and build your confidence in doing the job right the first time. After you work through the review questions, the problem-solving scenarios, the visual test, the thought-provoking "Consider This" section, and the fun and useful practice projects, you're well on your way to achieving your goal of working effectively with your health insurance plan.

Q&A

1. What is the term for the dollar amount you must pay before the insurance company pays?

   a. Deductible.
   b. Coinsurance.
   c. Fee-for-service.

2. What is a drug formulary?

   a. The recipe for mixing a prescription.
   b. A list of drugs to avoid.
   c. A list of drugs your health plan approves.

3. What is the purpose of a flexible spending account?

   a. To set aside pretax dollars to pay for health-related expenses.
   b. To set up a payment plan to pay overdue medical bills.
   c. To pay for workers' compensation insurance.

4. Health insurance plans use coordination of benefits to

   a. Set the reasonable and customary fees for medical procedures.
   b. Determine the amount of coinsurance you pay after you pay the deductible.
   c. Prevent duplication of benefits when you submit a claim to more than one insurance company.

5. COBRA is designed to

a. Protect policyholders covered under individual plans who may get insufficient coverage.

b. Protect employees covered under group plans who may lose their health insurance coverage.

c. Protect employees covered under group plans who may pay too much in medical expenses.

Answers: (1) a. (2) c. (3) a. (4) c. (5) b.

Scenarios

1. You are preparing to have major surgery. Your surgeon has told you that the operation will cost $2,300. You notify your health insurance company. Your insurer tells you that the reasonable and customary fee for this operation is $1,800 and that your benefits are based on this amount, which means that you are responsible for paying the difference. What are your options?

_____

_____

2. Your Medicare provider offers to write up a bill for medical tests that he didn't perform if you split the money you receive from Medicare with him. You should

_____

_____

Answers: (1) Ask your surgeon to accept the reasonable and customary fee as payment in full. If he or she won't, find another surgeon. (2) Report your doctor immediately to the Department of Health and Human Services.

Visual Test

When you're evaluating two health insurance plans, one of the factors to consider is what your minimum cost is before you're entitled to any benefits. Table R-1 compares monthly premiums and deductibles in two different group health insurance plans. Each plan shows premiums and deductibles for three possible family configurations: employee only, employee and one dependent, and employee and two or more dependents. To compare the two plans, calculate the minimum annual amounts that you would have to pay before the insurance company pays any benefits for medical expenses that you incur during a year. Fill in the blanks with these amounts.

Consider This

■ Did you know that Congress is considering new laws that relate to health insurance all the time? New laws can affect your benefits and treatment under your health insurance plan. Go to **http://thomas.loc.gov** on the Internet to see what Congress is doing about health insurance.

■ Did you know that you have the right to appeal a claim? Health insurance plans usually provide an established procedure for contesting benefits decisions. Following the procedure and submitting your appeal on time are important if you want the insurer to reconsider your claim. See Chapter 8 for more details.

Practice Projects

1. Design a form or use an existing one to create a personal health history for yourself. Fill in as much information as possible.

2. Review your current health plan and see whether you need to adjust coverage based on changes in your health, family status, budget, and other factors.

Table R-1:   Visual Test Table

Plan 1 Monthly Premium	Plan 1 Annual Deductible ($180 Per Individual/ $540 Per Family)	Plan 1 Minimum Outlay for One Year Before Benefits Are Paid	Plan 2 Monthly Premium	Plan 2 Annual Deductible ($1,200 Per Individual/ $3,600 Per Family)	Plan 2 Minimum Outlay for One Year Before Benefits Are Paid
$10 (employee only)	$180		None (employee only)	$1,200	
$100 (employee + 1 dependent)	$180 × 2		$9 (employee + 1 dependent)	$1,200 × 2	
$172 (employee + 2 or more dependents)	$540		$15 (employee + 2 or more dependents)	$3,600	

Answers: Plan 1 (top to bottom): $10 x 12 + $180 = $300; $100 x 12 + $360 = $1,560;
$172 x 12 + $540 = $2,604.
Plan 2 (top to bottom): $0 x 12 + $1,200 = $1,200; $9 x 12 + $2,400 = $2,508;
$15 x 12 + $3,600 = $3,780.

CLIFFSNOTES RESOURCE CENTER

The learning doesn't need to stop here. CliffsNotes Resource Center shows you the best of the best. You find here names, addresses, telephone numbers, and e-mail and Web addresses for many books, publications, and organizations related to health insurance. More awaits you at **www.cliffsnotes.com**.

Books

For some great next-step books, check out the following:

The Complete Guide to Health Insurance: How to Beat the High Cost of Being Sick, by Kathleen Hogue, Cheryl Jensen, and Kathleen McClurg Urban, gives you strategies to manage your health insurance, using real-life examples. Walker Publishing Company, Inc., 1988. $24.95

Health Care Choices for Today's Consumer, edited by Marc S. Miller, Ph.D., helps you make educated choices about health insurance. Living Planet Press, 1995. $17.95

Health Insurance: How to Get It, Keep It, or Improve What You've Got, 2nd ed., by Robert Enteen, Ph.D., helps you find, evaluate, and compare health insurance plans. Demos Vermande, 1996. $29.95

Medicare Made Simple A Consumer's Guide to the Medicare Program, by Denise Knaus, explains Medicare's major issues and helps make Medicare easy to use. Health Information Press, 1996. $14.95

Find these books in your favorite bookstores (on the Internet and at a store near you). We also have three Web sites that you can use to read about all the books that IDG Books Worldwide, Inc., publishes:

- **www.cliffsnotes.com**
- **www.dummies.com**
- **www.idgbooks.com**

Internet

Check out these Web sites for more information about health care topics:

Families USA Foundation, www.familiesusa.org/LINKS. HTM, sponsors this in-depth resource list and information clearinghouse on managed care.

The Consumer Insurance Guide, www.insure.com/health, provides information on spiritual care, mental health parity laws, and other insurance-related topics.

The Health Pages, www.thehealthpages.com/ar-hosps.html covers various topics. All Hospitals Are Not Created Equal helps you choose a hospital; Your Guide to Managed Care provides guidelines on choosing health care coverage; Health Care's Front Line: Primary Care Physicians helps you choose a primary care physician by state.

Next time you're on the Internet, don't forget to drop by **www.cliffsnotes.com**. We created an online Resource Center that you can use today, tomorrow, and beyond.

Other Media

Many organizations offer publications filled with helpful information on health insurance topics, such as the following:

Checkup on Health Insurance Choices helps you choose a health insurance plan that's right for you; *Choosing and Using a Health Plan* details health plan choices, benefits, costs, and suggestions for getting the most from your plan. Agency for

Health Care Policy and Research (AHCPR) and the National Council on Patient Information and Education, Rockville, MD, Publications Clearinghouse, P.O. Box 8547 Silver Spring, MD 20907; phone 800-358-9295; Web site **www.ahcpr.gov/consumer**

The Consumer's Guide to Disability Insurance helps you decide whether you need disability coverage and helps you compare policies. *The Consumer's Guide to Long-Term Care Insurance* explains what long-term care is, how long-term care insurance works and what it costs, and provides a checklist to compare policies. *The Consumer's Guide to Medicare Supplement Insurance; HIAA Consumer Information Guide to Health Insurance,* discusses the basic forms of health coverage and includes a checklist to help you compare plans. Health Insurance Association of America (HIAA), 555 13th St., N.W., Suite 600 East, Washington, D.C. 20004; Web site **www.hiaa.org**

Learning About Medicare Health Plans . . . Six Steps to Choosing a Medicare Health Plan, provides a worksheet for you to compare Medicare plans. Publication No. HCFA-10114, October 1998, Department of Health and Human Services (DHHS), Health Care Financing Administration (HCFA), 7500 Security Blvd., Baltimore, MD 21244-1850; Web site **www.medicare.gov/publications.html**

Managed Care: What Consumers Need to Know describes managed care, types of managed care plans, and a checklist to help you choose a plan. American Association of Retired Persons (AARP), 611 E St., N.W., Washington, D.C. 20049; phone 202-434-2277; Web site **www.aarp.org/monthly/managed care/home.html**

Resource Kit

Some of the organizations that may be able to provide you with assistance with health insurance concerns include the following:

Agency for Health Care Policy and Research (AHCPR), federal agency that sponsors and conducts research on the quality and outcomes of health care services. Executive Office Center, 2101 East Jefferson St., Rockville, MD 20852; phone 800-358-9295 (publications only), 301-594-2800 (fax-on-demand service — use a fax machine with a Touch-Tone telephone handset); TDD, hearing impaired only, 888-586-6340; Web site **www.ahcpr.gov/about/contacts.htm**

Health Care Financing Administration (HCFA) provides information about health plan benefits, rights, and options; Medigap insurance; quality of managed care plans; and the Medicare Plus Choice program. Phone 800-MEDICARE or 800-633-4227; TTY-TDD hearing- and speech-impaired 877-486-2048.

National Committee for Quality Assurance (NCQA) accredits HMOs and other managed care organizations. 2000 L St., N.W., Suite 500, Washington, D.C. 20036; phone 202-955-3500, fax 202-955-3599; 24-hour automated status line for plan accreditation information 888-275-7585; Web site **www.ncqa.org**

To find your state health insurance contact, check with the National Association of Insurance Commissioners, 120 W. 12th St., Suite 1100, Kansas City, MO 64105; phone 816-842-3600 or 816-374-7175; Web site **www.naic.org** or **www.insure.com/states**

Send Us Your Favorite Tips

In your quest for learning, have you ever experienced that sublime moment when you figure out a trick that saves time or trouble? Perhaps you realized you were taking ten steps to accomplish something that could have taken two. Or you've found a little-known workaround that gets great results. If you've discovered a useful tip that helped you navigate the maze of health insurance more effectively and you'd like to share it, the CliffsNotes staff would love to hear from you. Go to our Web site at **www.cliffsnotes.com** and click the Talk to Us button. If your tip is selected, we may publish it as part of CliffsNotes Daily, our exciting, free e-mail newsletter. To find out more or to subscribe to a newsletter, go to **www.cliffsnotes.com** on the Web.

INDEX

A

abortions, 34
accreditation, 106
acupuncture, 45
AIDS screening, 34
alternative care, 45–46
applications
    individual plans, 8
assignment of benefits, claim form, 85
automatic enrollment, Medicare, 70

B

basic coverage, 10–11
    hospital charges, 10
    hospitalization, 10
    physician expenses, 10
    surgical expenses, 10
beneficiary
    defined, 18
    Medicare beneficiary, 18
    qualified beneficiaries, 18
benefits
    Medicare, 71
    schedule of benefits, 38
blood pressure, 34
books, 114–115

C

cancer insurance. *See* dread disease
    policies
cancer screening, 34
cap, costs, 12
catastrophic coverage policy, 57–58
catastrophic limit, 25, 57–59
certification, 44–45
    surgery, outpatient, 39
cesarean deliveries, 34
checklist, 106–109
CHIP (Children's Health Insurance
    Program), 79
cholesterol screening, 34
claim forms, 12, 80–82
claim out period (FSA), 29

claims, 80–88
    appealing, 89–92
    assignment of benefits, 85
    COB (Coordination of Benefits),
        83–84
    recordkeeping, 80–82
    submitting, 85–88
closed formularies, prescription drugs,
    63
COB (Coordination of Benefits), 83–84
COBRA (Consolidated Omnibus
    Budget Reconciliation Act), 19–20
coinsurance, 12, 24–25
    defined, 5
    total annual, 13
coinsurance, 23. *See also* copayments
complementary care, 45
comprehensive coverage, 10
conditionally renewable policies, 8
confidentiality, 94–97
consumer protection, 94–97
consumer rights, 94–99
continuation, defined, 18
continuing coverage, 18–20
    COBRA, 19–20
    conversion options, 19
conversion options, 19
conversion, defined, 18
Coordination of Benefits (COB), 83–84
copayments, 23
    defined, 6
    prescription drugs, 64
costs, 12–13, 21–27, 29–32
    cap, 12
    copayments, 23
    covered charges, 21
    deductibles, 24–25
    dread disease policies, 56
    individual plans, 8–9
    limiting expenses, 25–26
    premiums, 21–23
    pretax dollars, 27, 29
    reasonable and customary, 10
    reasonable and customary fees, 30–32
coverage, 33–46
    acupuncture, 45
    alternative care, 45–46
    basic, 10–11
    critical illness, 57
    dental care, 48, 50–52
    dependents, 101–102

COMING SOON FROM CLIFFSNOTES

Online Shopping

HTML

Choosing a PC

Beginning Programming

Careers

Windows 98 Home Networking

eBay Online Auctions

PC Upgrade and Repair

Business

Microsoft Word 2000

Microsoft PowerPoint 2000

Finance

Microsoft Outlook 2000

Digital Photography

Palm Computing

Investing

Windows 2000

Online Research

IDG
BOOKS
WORLDWIDE

...Bay

Hav... ...incredible
barg... ...t people are
wil... ...ne garbage?
If... ...st auc-
tio... *Selling*
on... ...You'll
le...

■ ...toys to

■ ...s at the

■

■ ...bidders

■

F... ...ffsNotes
l...

...the bot-
...itself is

...vord and
...e appears
...y submit
...click the

...ou return
⇨Reload
(Netscape Navigator) or View⇨Refresh (Microsoft Internet Explorer) to reload the Web page information. Your
new high bid appears on the Web page, and your name
appears as the high bidder.